Dedication

To my dear wife who is the delight of my life. She has always been the best part of me! I am grateful for her enthusiastic support of my adventurist spirit for these 50+ years.

She shared in many of these stories. Without her encouragement this book would have forever remained a dream. God fashioned her just for me and I'm so glad He sent her along in my lifetime.

Table of Contents

Foreword

Being married to Bob for over 50 years has been a continuing adventure. I have learned to be flexible because he is as unpredictable as he is lovable. He is a doting parent and grandparent who loves and encourages his offspring. You cannot be around my husband very long before everyone is laughing. Let me share one example: It has been a tradition in our family to have a snack before retiring. One evening, the whole family came home late from a huge dinner. Everyone was stuffed. Bob was uncomfortably full, he collapsed in his chair and announced to all, "How in the world am I going to be able to ram a snack down my throat?"

For a farm girl who never ventured far from home, going to California on our honeymoon opened my eyes to the future. He has expanded my horizons as I have accompanied him on many of the exciting stories you are about to read. Our two daughters and I saw a book in his future long before he did. One thing I must emphasize! Being married to Bob has been many things, but one thing is certain, LIFE HAS NEVER BEEN DULL.

About the Book

You may wonder, with at least a trillion books written on every subject from aardvarks to zymurgy, why in the world would anyone want to write another book? Well, I can think of only three valid reasons. First, to satisfy a severely inflated ego. Many years ago I suffered from this disease but until recently it had been in remission. Suddenly, it has recurred. The good news is that my medication is apparently working since I now don't think I am as great as I once thought I was. The second valid reason I decided to write this book is I have a great story to tell. Now if only I could remember what it was! But the third and most important reason I decided to write this book now is at the rate I'm losing brain cells, I had better get to it because at the present rate, I have senility scheduled in mid-October.

If I am anything, and the jury has not returned a verdict on that, I am a storyteller. Even when I return from Wal-mart, my wife will say, "I know there's a story about your trip. What is it?" I love to tell stories! That's exactly what this book is all about. Many years ago, I received a book from my daughter. It was a beautifully bound book of blank pages. She said, "Daddy, with all of your stories, some day you need to write a book." What you are holding in your hand is the response to that gift.

This book is not an autobiography. It is a compilation of personal short stories. Every one of these stories is true. I know that because I have lived each one. Many of my experiences will make you laugh. Several are suspense filled. Some will display an incredible amount of naiveté and or unabashed stupidity. Many of these stories are of such genuine human interest that you may very well wish you could have lived them along with me. Some of the stories may seem to appeal to men more than to women, i.e. hunting stories, etc., but ladies, don't pass over these stories. You may learn just how difficult it is to be a man.

These stories are deliberately and randomly chosen so as to be in no chronological order since my entire life has been out of chronological order. To the very best of my ability, together with outside confirmation when available, I have attempted to be factually accurate and avoid exaggeration. Fortunately for many of the stories, especially the various trips reported on, I have relied on diaries, itineraries, and fellow witnesses. However, without doing injury to the efficacy of the story, I have injected my own personality into each description. You will quickly learn that I have a mind that is severely warped. (The direct result of too many hot showers.)

To be perfectly honest and forthright, this book has limited socially redeemable qualities. It is purposely lighthearted and designed to entertain, not necessarily inform. I readily admit, my primary purpose in telling any story is to make people either laugh or at least feel better about themselves and their circumstances. In the Bible, Solomon, the wisest man who ever lived said, "There is a time to laugh!" I propose in these days of uncertainty, that time is now.

If you laugh a lot, when you get older, all your wrinkles will be in the right places.

For maximum benefit, as you read each story, put yourself in my place. Live the story vicariously through me. My hope is that you will see how invigorating life can be. I encourage you to break out of any negative view of your environment, and challenge the unknown, search out all possibilities, and never fear taking the road less traveled. I encourage you to create your own opportunities to do things you have never done before. It will add zest to your life.

It was Mark Twain who said, "Years from now, you will be more disappointed by the things you didn't do than by the things you did. So throw off the bowlines, and sail away from the safe harbor. Catch the trade winds in your sails. Explore! Dream! Discover!"

Remember, life is like a mirror. For best results, smile at it. If you do, I know you will discover, as I have, that God designed life to be enjoyed. Make every day count. I encourage you to try to learn one new thing each day. You'll feel better, you'll look better, and you will have friends to spare. Count on it!

Finally, I must warn you, I have never written anything longer than my name. The success of this effort will depend entirely on your exceptional ability as a reader. (Did you notice how cleverly I shifted the responsibility of the success of this book from me to you?)

I am particularly excited now! This book is already in its third printing. I know that, because I printed the three copies myself.

I sincerely hope you will enjoy the real-life stories, that could really have happened to anyone, they just happened to happen to me. So come along, we've got some living to do!

About the Author

Hello! My name is Robert Price Nace. I was born in 1931, in the midst of the Great Depression, but the depression was not my fault. My parents were Horace and Lydia Nace. My father died when I was only one year old. I could never understand why I did not have a daddy like my friends had. I am the fourth child in a family of four children. My parents were determined to produce a boy after failing three times. I have three sisters.

I grew up believing sisters were like pets. Every boy should have a couple! You could really enjoy them, you could play with them, and you could chase them with worms. My one sister has a scar on her arm attesting to just how much fun you can have with three sisters. I know how much my sisters looked forward to these contests but they seemed to lack the ability to express their joy.

I graduated from Souderton High School with honors (that's Bill Honors, a good friend, I'll never forget him) in the class of '49, that's 1949. I skipped college and began working on my Doctorate program at Peter Becker Retirement Community. I know every doctor in the place.

I am married to the only girl who could have survived this marriage. Mildred is such an integral part of who I am that it is scary. She sometimes can finish my sentences! Often she does that in order to correct the mistake I've already made in the first part of the sentence. I am like the goose who flies around and makes all the noise but let there be no mistake, she is the wind beneath my wings.

We have two daughters, two sons-in-law, five grandchildren and as of this writing, one great-grandson. If I had a dog, which sadly I don't, his name would be inserted here. If I had a cat, her name would be omitted here since I have no fondness for cats.

I am the product of small-town America. I grew up with my family in several small rural communities in southeastern Pennsylvania. Towns so small, that if you sneezed, you could hear a chorus of "geshundheits." Several of my hometowns were so small that if you saw a cute young thing dining with a man old enough to be her father, he was. I could write a book about the things that happened in my hometowns. Oh wait, that's what I am doing!

Being a depression baby, without a father in the home, you can imagine we were dirt poor. But nobody told me. I thought everybody ate pretzel soup for supper, with one cup of hot water to two cups of milk. I didn't know, nor did it matter to me, that some of the clothes I wore had been worn first by some other little boy. To ask for help, especially from the government, to my mother would be unthinkable. In those good old days lots of practical help came from church families and from neighbors in our communities. Neighbor helping neighbor is an American tradition that made us as a nation, the truly great nation we are.

Growing up, we were proud and faithful members of the Vernfield Church of the Brethren. Since my mother had limited experience in raising a boy, her strategy was to take this kid to church whenever the doors were open. I attended more ladies' sewing circle meetings than I care to remember. But I do have many happy memories of that church. Lasting friendships were built there. I was baptized there. The Church of the Brethren's form of baptism was by full immersion. It was their practice to use a small stream adjacent to the church. I can clearly recall watching the ministers break the ice in order to baptize believers. I was baptized in July! Growing up, Sunday was a special day for our family and our community. A day of limited activity. A day to visit friends and families. A day to sit on the porch on rockers and reflect. I recall being the worst reflector. I wanted to do anything but reflect, even to the point where I was willing to consider civil disobedience if I had known what that was. The only exception was a visit to my grandparents whose house was next to the trolley tracks. Did you know that if you put a penny on the track, after the trolley goes by, you have a huge penny? Worthless but huge!

Reflecting on my growing up days in church, there is one regret I remember fondly. As an early teenager, I was permitted to sit in the back row of the church during the Sunday morning preaching service along with other teenagers. Why my mother permitted this I will never know. It had the ingredients of a major train wreck. One of our number was gifted at drawing cartoons. He would pass them down the row and I would put captions on them. On more than one occasion the minister would need to stop in the middle of his sermon to reprimand the back row. At such times, I would get a look from my mother that could melt glass. I could also interpret that look. It said, "Son, for the sake of your continued good health, I would suggest you run away from home at your earliest possible convenience."

I have always maintained that growing up in small rural towns helped to shape my core values, build my principle of self determination, and my commitment to be all God created me to be. My philosophy of life is simple. Concern myself less with what I don't have, celebrate what I have been given by God, and recognize His desire that I enjoy what He has given. I love to laugh, and I enjoy trying to make others laugh. I try to see the humor in everyday circumstances. The Bible tells us that "laughter does a body good like medicine."

According to a book called *Healing Through Humor*, written by Charles & Frances Hunter, here is what happens when you laugh:

- Your heart & lungs are stimulated.
- Your heart beats faster & your blood pressure rises temporarily.
- You breathe deeper & oxygenate more blood.
- Your body releases endorphins, your own natural pain killers, and you produce more immune cells.
- You burn seventy-eight times as many calories as you would in a resting state.
- Your diaphragm, facial muscles and internal organs all get bounced around in a massage sometimes referred to as "internal jogging".
- After a hearty laugh, your muscles and arteries relax. That's great for easing pain. It also aids digestion.

I rest my case!

The Sins of an Adolescent

CHAPTER 1

I grew up without a father. That meant that in the summer-time, I usually went to live with various farm families from our church. While I missed my family in those days, I enjoyed spending time on a farm. A boy can learn a lot of things on a farm that he cannot learn in any other way. For example:

- I learned it is not good to pee on an electric fence.
- I learned that cows are inherently stupid. If you forget to close the gate, they will walk out.
- I learned that chickens do not give up their eggs without a fight.
- I learned that cows can kick.
- I learned the most fun a boy can have on a farm is to ride on a tractor.
- I learned that farmers put ice cream on their cereal and eat cake for breakfast.
- I learned that pigs stink.
- I learned there is always something around a farm that's broken.

- I learned that cleaning out the cow stable
  is not all it is cracked up to be.
- I learned that farm families get fully
  dressed in a late night thunderstorm,
  in the event of a lightning strike and animals needing to be evacuated.

I spent one summer with my aunt and uncle on their small farm. They had three boys, so the four of us were licensed to create havoc. We had pillow fights that could qualify as Olympic events. Fighting of any kind, while not sanctioned, was permitted with one house rule: at the first sight of blood, a truce had to be declared. We did everything we could do to keep from bleeding.

My uncle was a very strict disciplinarian. You'd do well to obey his commands! He once gave me a small bucket and told me to fill it two-thirds full of water. My math skills had not yet been invented so I did not have a clue what two-thirds full was. I trembled at the thought that I didn't know. Fortunately, I have a natural genius that kicks in just for such times of dire necessity. I filled the bucket to the top and told him he could pour water out until he got to two-thirds.

My uncle had prized chickens—he called them banty roosters. They were mildly colorful, and he enjoyed them. I don't know what their creative purpose was, they didn't lay eggs and we didn't eat them: They just strutted around the barnyard. My uncle also had an apple tree. You may wonder what a banty rooster and an apple tree have in common. Please be patient, I'm about to tell you. I found banty roosters make great targets. Little green apples make the combination complete. Targets and apples are all you need.

On one particular day, I thought my arm strength had reached its maximum and my delivery form had never been better. So I took dead aim and fired a missile directly at the target in front of me. My shot was better than I had expected. The apple hit the banty rooster right on the side of the head. The rooster squawked, stumbled, and then fell over. I had not expected this result. Now, what to do . . . what to do? I could go and confess my sin and take the consequences but that was too extreme. The only option was to bury the evidence. I quickly grabbed the rooster by the leg, carried it to the barn and prepared to get a shovel for the burial. By the time I returned to the rooster with my shovel, it had revived and ran away. I quickly put the shovel back and sang all four stanzas of the Hallelujah Chorus.

On one occasion, we were encouraged to go to a neighboring farm where the farmer grew tomatoes. We were promised ten cents for every basket of tomatoes we picked. I had just finished my first basket of tomatoes. (Now, I want the record to show, I did not throw the first tomato.) Soon after that, I received a tomato right in the back of my neck. I did not overreact, I preferred to be a spectator to what I knew was the coming event. After the second tomato struck, I felt obligated to enter the fray. Tomatoes filled the air and none of them were destined for the baskets. Before it had barely begun, our picking season was over. Here is the worst part: We were invited to leave the farm and never to return, but I never received the dime I had legitimately earned. But I must add, you have not enjoyed life to the full until you have survived a full-blown tomato fight.

• • • • •

Now, the worst story I truly hesitate to tell! Believe me, I still tremble at reflecting on what could have been. If there are any boys around ten years of age in the room while you are reading this story, it might be best if they left the room.

Long before there was waste management, or recycling, there was a common method of disposing of junk you no longer wanted. It was called a "dump." Most farms had one. They were most often off in some ravine and out of sight. They were terrific places for a young boy to search and see what he could find.

One day, as I was searching for treasure, I found a rusty single barrel shotgun. No stock, just a barrel. I picked it up and contemplated what a boy could do with such a find. I had a very bad idea. No one was home except my one cousin who had good common sense, so I couldn't tell him what I had in mind.

What I decided to do is the worst possible course of action. I had no idea there were gauges to shotguns. Was this a 12-gauge, a 16-gauge or a 20-gauge? I didn't know but it didn't make any difference to me. I knew my uncle kept his guns in the barn, and I assumed I could find a gun shell. I did. I put it into the barrel of the gun and it fit. I took a hammer, a large nail, and the barrel with the shell inserted out to the cement area where there was a hand water pump. I put a small piece of wood at the opposite end of the barrel so I could tell if anything came out. I laid the barrel on the cement, put my left foot on the barrel, aimed the nail on the center of the shell, and swung the hammer. There was a deafening roar. The majority of the force came out the back of the barrel. It knocked me over, the hammer flew backward, and temporarily I lost my sense of hearing. For a substantial period of time, there was a constant ringing in my ears that gradually faded. My cousin heard the shot and came running to see what it was. I told him what I had done, but I swore him to secrecy. To the best of my knowledge, he took our secret to his grave.

All the possibilities of what could have happened are absolutely frightening. Most assuredly there is a God who protects those whose common sense has completely left their body.

My Eating Disorder

CHAPTER 2

I readily admit to a substantial issue regarding mealtimes. For some unknown reason I cannot maintain a clean and tidy place at the table. For example, when the meal has concluded, it looks as though the other guests haven't eaten—everything clean, tools of the trade nicely aligned, water glass clear and sparkling.

Why is it not like that at my place? For all practical purposes, it appears I have not employed a plate. I just put the food right on the tablecloth. It looks like the aftermath of a tsunami. My water glass contains remnants of the entire menu. My napkin is not only on the floor, it is under the feet of the people at the next table. You can bet there is a cherry tomato rolling somewhere under the table. There is another absolute: At some point during the meal, my wife will say, "Honey, you keep dragging your sleeve through the gravy." If we have pancakes with syrup, I do not need to hold my fork, as it is permanently attached to my thumb and forefinger. My knife is stuck fast to the palm of my left hand. It is not a problem at home because my wife puts a 9 x 12 canvas under my chair to protect the carpet in the living room. I have tried to analyze why this problem continues. I, personally, believe it is caused by my being partially deaf in my left ear.

This may be the appropriate place to also discuss my food preferences. I am not that complicated. I am simply a meat and potatoes kind of a guy. In meat, I like beef in any form. I like my steaks medium rare. I will eat chicken if it isn't fried. I prefer dark meat, no skin. I will eat a pig if it is in the form of crisp bacon. I stopped enjoying sausage when someone told me it was the small intestine of the pig stuffed with what was rejected by the garbage disposal. I am very careful about ham since long ago I ordered a ham and the butcher suggested a cured ham. Cured? Wow! What did it have?

I enjoy seafood as long as it is not fish. Lobster and steamed clams are particular favorites because I really like melted butter. I enjoy oysters in most forms but raw oysters require a pint of cocktail sauce per oyster. I do make one exception to my otherwise reasonable approach to food. I enjoy hard shell crabs found along the eastern shore of Maryland. If you have ever sat down and looked a crab in the eye, saw legs coming out from everywhere and still concluded this thing is edible, you are ready for the challenge of ripping this thing apart. If you suffer from any matters of the heart, it may be best to buy your crab meat by the pound.

Now, with respect to vegetables, I will state right up front I have no respect for vegetables. I enjoy potatoes in any form: baked, stuffed, hashed, smashed, diced, boiled, scalloped, fried, shredded, French fried, or hanging on a rope. Soon after we were married, my wife and I went to a very nice restaurant. I ordered prime rib, and the waiter asked me what two vegetables I would like. I told him I would like a baked potato and French fries. Both my wife and the waiter went into uncontrollable convolutions. Both clearly overreacted. He asked what I would like and I told him. Well, they created such a scene! I could have shot someone in that restaurant and received less attention. I was later informed that I had committed a sin for which there is no pardon.

My wife and I have this constant argument. She insists that a proper serving on a plate requires color. I don't see why. I'm not doing a painting here, I'm just going to eat this stuff. She thinks broccoli looks really good on the plate. I have looked at broccoli under a soft light, under glass, in the dark and hanging on the wall, and I do not see beauty anywhere. She thinks orange adds color and suggests carrots. She insists that carrots are not only colorful, they are nutritious and good for your eyes. I respond, "Good for your eyes, really? Then how come I see so many dead rabbits on the highway?"

I refuse to eat any casserole. The ingredients are completely unidentifiable. I discovered long ago that casseroles are but a devious scheme that could only be contrived by a wife set on force feeding vegetables to unsuspecting husbands. A word to all wives—we may have been born at night—but it wasn't last night.

MY OPPOSITION TO EXERCISE

While I'm reflecting on certain foods I can do without, there are a few other things I find offensive. For example, exercise, what good is it? If I'm going to walk, I want to go somewhere. To start at home and end at home seems futile. Even worse is a treadmill. There you walk and you don't even move. You stop where you started. How dumb is that? Anyway, there is nothing more embarrassing than being on a treadmill at a reasonable speed, and some young thing next to you is running at top speed. One of these days I'm pulling the plug on her machine. I have a paid membership at the local YMCA, but I only go when I have exhausted all valid reasons for not going. Besides, I maintain that exercise at the Y makes you fat because I only see fat people there. That brings me to those machines designed by masochists to help you tone your muscles. My muscles are tone deaf, and I see no ill effects. I remember the guy who died jogging. I cannot take that chance. Besides, I have never heard of anyone who ever rested to death.

AND A FEW OTHER THINGS

My wife has a few strange quirks that confuse me a bit. For example, she has this paranoia about making our bed the very first thing in the morning. However, it is not true that if I get up in the middle of the night to go to the bathroom, when I return my side of the bed has been made. I believe her rationale for making the bed is if a burglar breaks into our house while we are gone, she would be embarrassed if the burglar saw an unmade bed. Why is this such a big deal to me? Because I believe making the bed in the morning is a total waste of time. At night, you crawl right back in bed, so why bother. If I lived alone (which I hope I never do) I would make the bed once a month—maybe.

In addition, my wife is so insistent that I wear clean underwear every day that she lays out my clothes for the next day. So that you don't think I'm a perfect slob, I too insist on clean underwear. However, I suspect her rationale for clean underwear for me, is if I were involved in an accident, she would not want the paramedics thinking her husband didn't wear clean underwear.

• • • • •

To be fair, I have a few quirks of my own but mine are far more reasonable. For example, if I go somewhere, it is against my own law to return the same way I traveled originally. My rationale: I already saw everything on the first trip, why would I look at it again.

They say you can tell a lot about a person by their pet peeves. Well, I admit to having a few pet peeves like:

Why is it when you are late, every traffic light is red? When time is of no concern, every traffic light is green.

I would love to get my hands on the guy who invented adult-proof plastic packages. To open these packages requires two knives, a hammer, and maybe a gun. By the time you get the thing out of its tomb, you are minus three fingernails, you have a blood blister on your elbow and you have grown to hate the item that five minutes before you couldn't do without it.

Why is it, you wait in line at Burger King for thirty minutes, then finally, the person in front of you gets to the counter and it's only then they begin to think about what they may wish to order?

You are in a restaurant. The service is exemplary. Your order is taken promptly, your food arrives quickly, the wait staff comes, and asks you seven times if everything is satisfactory. You are finished with your meal, but you age waiting for the check while your wait staff takes their leave of absence.

Why is it that when you call the customer service department of every company, the person whose job it is to assist you is totally unfamiliar with the English language? If I wanted to talk to someone in Bombay, I would have called them directly.

Why is it that the paint chip you selected at the paint store bears little resemblance to the color of your living room wall?

Do you remember when you would call a place of business and someone would answer "Hello?" Now when you call you get:

> For English push 1 . . .
> For personnel directory push 2
> For billing push 3
> For accounts receivable push 4
> On and on, and on, then you finally,
> To hear your options again push 7

In the mean time there was no option for the reason you called: It is here I wish they would say, "This call may be recorded for training purposes." Thank goodness my call is very important to them or who knows how long this annoying, antagonizing, irritating procedure would take. By the time you finally get a live person to speak to you, you have grown so old you can't remember why you called.

People who leave their turn signals on forever: In the retirement community where I live, this is known as the eventual left turn. They reason, probably, at some point in time, down the road, I may want to turn left so I want to be prepared.

Where does it say that speed bumps need to be a foot high? Besides speed bump is a complete misnomer. They impede your speed.

My First Honeymoon

CHAPTER 3

The excitement in this marriage began long before the honeymoon.

I knew I had a winner on our very first date. When I took her home, we sat in my car with the radio on low, talking just to get to know each other. We seemed to be kindred spirits. After walking her to the front door and saying good night, I returned to my car and found the battery was not strong enough to start the car. What a great first impression! I had few options. I had to go back in and explain my plight. Without hesitation, she got her father's car, gently gave my car a push down the drive and off I went! I knew right then, this girl was a "keeper."

We had a great courtship and since things were progressing nicely, I thought the time had come for me to at least consider marriage. The night I proposed was indeed memorable. I asked her if she would marry me. She said she would be happy to marry me. Immediately, I developed a severe nose bleed. I was wearing a light blue blazer and it was covered in blood. What caused that reaction is clearly unknown, however, I have never enjoyed a nose bleed so much. I wanted to enshrine the jacket without cleaning as a memorial to one of my better days. (But that was vetoed!)

So in May, of 1952 or '53, Mildred Derstine and Robert Nace said "I do," and we did. From what I remember of the wedding, it wasn't all that bad. Some thought the bride in her beautiful gown looked stunning, while the groom looked stunned. Little did I know it would turn out to be the best day of my entire life.

Fortunately for me, I married a farmer's daughter. Someone who had never been farther from home than Broad Street. I had a plan to go to California before marriage but that plan failed. So anxious was I to go west that I suggested California for our honeymoon. While she was cautious, she was ready to go. I'll never forget, right after the wedding reception, with $400.00 in our pocket and stars in our eyes we set out for four weeks. Three weeks out and back and one week in southern California should be just about right. My mother had a brother and a sister and their spouses living in California. They didn't know it yet, but they were about to have guests.

I decided I would spare no expense to give my bride a first-class cabin for our first night away from home. We stopped in Lancaster, Pennsylvania, and as I promised, I spared no expense as that first night lodging cost $7.00. I'm proud to say that was the most I paid for lodging in four weeks. The room was palatial, hot and cold running water, and all the comforts you might expect for seven bucks.

We headed west and traveled the most famous road of that day, Route 66. We did get our kicks on Route 66. From the high point of our cabin in Lancaster, our lodging tended to go downhill. This was particularly true in the southwest. In New Mexico we paid $3.00 for a room so small the mice had to walk upright. In one motel, we had hot and cold water but the cold came right after you ran out of hot which was almost instantly. In this motel, the closet was a row of nails. In one motel in Flagstaff, Arizona, I needed to show my wedding ring before he would allow me to sign the register. The manager thought we looked too young.

My biggest concern was the desert. Our car had no air conditioning. Even before we reached the desert, it was unbearably hot. To drive with the windows closed was like riding in a wood stove. To drive with the windows open was akin to a blast furnace. As we approached the desert, I inquired at a service station just what I might expect in crossing this barren land. He asked if I intended to drive during the day. I replied. "Yes, of course. Is that a problem?" He said "Well, I wouldn't do it! I would sleep during the day and travel at night. It is much cooler and much less traffic." That did sound like a reasonable solution to us, and that's what I planned to do.

As we got closer to the desert, I decided on a second opinion. I inquired at a station that had a huge sign, LAST GAS BEFORE DESERT. What better counsel could I get than from someone so close to the action? I relayed my night driving plan to the attendant and asked for his opinion. His comment was. "That's alright if you don't mind getting held up at gun point and robbed by highway bandits." Oh, boy! I asked what he would recommend and he said we could travel during the day without difficulty if we had a water bag. A what? A bag to carry water! Well, I had never heard of such a thing and I was rapidly becoming suspicious of a lot of his suggestions. We were just kids after all, and clearly vulnerable. Nonetheless, by this time I was getting to enjoy my new lifestyle and didn't want to put it in jeopardy at the point of a gun. I asked him to tell me about this water bag phenomenon. It is a canvas bag that you fill with water and hang on the hood ornament of the car. As you travel, the evaporation will keep the water cool enough to drink. And the best news of all was that he just happened to sell them. Overwhelmed by this stroke of good fortune, we bought a water bag. I filled it with water, I hung it over the hood ornament of the car as per the instructions. One hour later, I stopped and checked the water bag. Yup, it was empty and the bag was stone dry! There is one born every minute. Sadly, I was the one for that minute.

As I stated, my mother had a brother and his wife, and a sister and her husband living in southern California: Uncle Melvin and Aunt Mildred and Aunt Minnie and Uncle Cyrus.

I did not know for sure, but I highly suspected that my mother had called each one and asked them to look out for us and after us. We arrived in Los Angeles in mid-afternoon and after some searching came to the home of our first victim, Uncle Melvin and Aunt Mildred. I could not remember if I had ever met them, but I surely would not know what they looked like or what to expect. I rang the bell. A big person came to the door. I, very hesitantly, inquired, "Uncle Melvin?" "No, I'm your Aunt Mildred." Not a great start given that my next question was going to be. "Will you feed us, and can we bunk here for a few days?" But, if you saw the size of my Aunt Mildred, and her attire, you would agree that it was an honest mistake. (However, it is not true that she once played linebacker for UCLA.) She invited us in and agreed to make supper. The toasted cheese sandwiches were good. We found out toasted cheese sandwiches were her specialty. They were also the extent of her culinary genius.

We had traveled all day and were ready for a good night's sleep. Unfortunately, Uncle Melvin brought out a punch bowl filled to the brim with 35 mm slides. No order, no interest, no good! After an hour of viewing people we didn't know and only from the knees down, I fell asleep. I often woke myself up with a snoring grunt. I reasoned being burned at the stake sounded like a fair option. Fortunately, my continuing snoring gave Uncle Melvin a clue, and we went off to bed.

The next day, Uncle Melvin insisted he wanted to take us down to Tijuana, Mexico, for a good, old-fashioned Mexican dinner. I don't enjoy any food that is more spicy than Cheerios, but the opportunity to actually go to Mexico had great appeal. He ordered dinner for all of us. Our meal consisted of a bowl of jalapeno peppers and I don't think much else. My hair turned flaming orange, it felt like my body was being consumed on the inside. My body fat melted and my toes were too hot to touch. Flaming darts of fire came out of every opening in my body. I was sweating a river. I thought, here I am dying in Mexico and my new bride will inherit my car, my only possession. I know my uncle would have shown more compassion for my plight, but he was too busy rolling on the floor in laughter. As you might reason, I did not particularly enjoy Mexico. However, I didn't get angry, but I did get even. The following day, just for spite, I ate two of Aunt Mildred's toasted cheese sandwiches.

We also visited with Uncle Cyrus and Aunt Minnie, two delightful older people. Very fatherly and motherly and we enjoyed our stay with them. One problem. When we drove with either of them around their community, we quickly discovered there were some driving issues. Uncle Cyrus's top speed we would call "park." He was stopped by the LAPD for going too slow on the California freeway. The officer said. "Sir, if you don't mend your ways, you will not be permitted on these freeways." He promised the officer he would take his demands under advisement. We coasted away from the officer.

Aunt Minnie on the other hand, did not suffer from the same malady as her husband. My Aunt Minnie became a totally different personality behind the wheel. Her mind-set was, that the safest way to get from point A to point B was to get there as rapidly as possible. She didn't drive the car, she just aimed it. She smashed the accelerator to the floor where it remained permanently lodged. She also must have suffered from dyslexia. She never stopped at any STOP sign. She must have read those signs as POTS, and she saw no reason to stop at POTS signs. On more than one occasion, people would blow their horn, slam on their brakes, with tires screaming to avoid contact. When they screamed obscenities, she thought they were just being friendly, and she would wave back. Nothing fazed her since she was totally oblivious to anything that happened around her. She was also one of these drivers, the faster she talked, the faster she drove. She would drive great distances while conversing and making eye contact with Mildred in the back seat.

We were rapidly running out of days here in fantasy land. But we had to dip our feet in the Pacific, had to have lunch on Rodeo Drive and had to complete the tourist scene. It was now time to get back to reality! We left California in great spirits, heading home via Las Vegas. As innocent as we were, we found it fascinating that the town was lit up and alive at night and a ghost town during the day. We must have been the only people walking vertically who did not "invest" a dime in their favorite form of entertainment. In those days in Vegas, they were still using almost exclusively silver dollars. If you walked around with twenty dollars in your pocket, you walked leaning over. In a rain storm you could drown.

We returned to Pennsylvania to enjoy life as newlyweds. We even had money left over from the $400.00! That's the good news. The other good news was that all our money was now in silver dollars. When my bride went shopping, she could only carry two dollars at a time.

A honeymoon can be a very memorable experience and it can have significant educational value. For example, in just four short weeks, I had learned a whole new language. It's called, "Yes dear."

Panic Comes Before Flying

CHAPTER 4

Several years ago, on our return flight from Florida to Allentown, Pennsylvania, we needed to change planes in Philadelphia. The flight from Philadelphia to Allentown is a very short hop by plane, less than an hour of flight time. The plane that was used for such a short flight was a small twin engine commuter type that seated about 25 people, with one row of seats on each side of the aircraft. Although my wife and I have flown all over the world, I confess to being sort of a white knuckle flyer. This trip was going to be particularly challenging for me! I tend not to trust any plane that you board by walking across the tarmac and climbing the steps. I prefer the tube form of entry.

On boarding, we were greeted warmly by the single flight attendant and shown to our assigned seats. My seat was on the right side of the aircraft, Row 1, Seat 1. I was seated directly behind the Captain separated by a curtain which was mostly open. I was bothered immediately, by the fact there was no Captain. Weren't they supposed to be on the plane checking a flight plan or throwing switches or something before passengers arrive? I was hoping they were not expecting a passenger to volunteer to be Captain.

Soon, a middle-aged man in a captain's uniform came up the aisle and seated himself right in front of me. Because of the curtain, I couldn't see what he was doing, but just having him there calmed my nerves. Following right behind him was a girl in a captain's uniform. I assumed this girl was older than she looked, but I thought she could pass for a teenager. She took her seat in the other captain's chair. Now, my heart stood dead still. I am not a male chauvinist (my wife won't permit it) but having this young girl in that seat was flat out frightening. I immediately bowed my head and said. "Lord, you can do this! Please make the man the flying captain, and the young girl the trainee. Amen."

As soon as the woman was seated, she opened the satchel she brought on board and took out a loose-leaf binder. She began to read, turning pages and throwing switches. Another check, another flicked switch. She was reading and flicking, and it did not look good to me. After another check and a flicked switch, the propeller right outside my window began to slowly rotate. It seemed extraordinarily reluctant, like it was winding up a huge rubber band. Slowly it gained momentum and became more enthusiastic. The plane began to tremble. The noise was deafening. As I watched that propeller spinning a few feet from me, I thought if it flies off, I am toast! I began to hypothesize about the maintenance of these small planes. I convinced myself that small planes got checked only if the support crew had time. I just hoped that the propeller was on tight enough.

About that time, there was another flick and the engine on the left side began to come to life. That motor repeated the whole exercise. Now the entire plane was in tumult. The whole thing reminded me of a woman in labor giving birth to twins. I had no view of what the male captain was doing; I only hoped he was paying attention, and I figured a little prayer wouldn't do any harm. Then the flight attendant began the standard pre-take off warning. I figured I had better listen to this one. She does not need to tell me where the EXIT door is. I have been thinking about that door ever since I got on board. She tells us our seat cushions are flotation devices. Wait a minute . . . there is no water between Philadelphia and Allentown. What good is a flotation device if you crash into a corn field? What's more, she never mentioned oxygen masks. I looked up, no oxygen. That convinced me this was an economy model plane. This discourse did very little to allay any of my flight concerns. Then she added, "Enjoy your flight to Allentown." What is she nuts? How could I enjoy this flight when a child was flying?

To my dismay, the female captain put on her head-set and began to talk. I could not hear what she was saying, but it sounded a lot like the Lord's Prayer. Slowly, the plane began to move. She was too short to see through the windshield, she had to look out the side window. Would somebody get a pillow for her to sit on for goodness sake? If something was ahead of her, she would see it after she hit it. What kind of sense does that make? We began to wind our way making rights and lefts and for what seemed like twenty minutes we were still on the ground. I assumed she was looking for a highway and we would drive to Allentown. Soon we came to a complete stop. Suddenly, those little engines that could began to roar. Down the runway we raced, and lo and behold, we were airborne. I began to try to remove my fingers which had been firmly embedded in the arm rests.

Very soon, the flight attendant announced preparations for landing at the Allentown International Airport. I recognized several familiar landmarks. For the first time I began to relax. Our plane touched down with such grace, it was hard to tell if we were on the ground. The landing was feather smooth. Sometimes those landings are so hard, it is difficult to know if we hit the ground or we were shot down.

I wanted to applaud and jump up and give this captain a great big giant hug but I didn't. I didn't want her to think I didn't trust her.

Alaska—The Last Frontier

As a boy, I was fascinated with Alaska. I would watch Western movies with the covered wagons heading west with their families and dream about what it must have been like. My wife says if I had been born in the 1800's instead of the 1900's, I would have been in one of those covered wagons. I believe she's right. I saw Alaska as an opportunity to experience what it might have been like to go west, young man! I just had to go and see!

The year was 1964, the year of the Alaskan Earthquake. An event that changed Alaska forever. They had just finished the Alaskan pipeline and I knew Alaska was about to move into the 20th century. I remembered reading their plans to pave and upgrade the intriguing Alaskan Highway. Before they did that, I just had to go. What follows is an attempt to relive those six weeks in 1966 when we, as a family, set out to take on America's last frontier.

I had a station wagon and we rented a seventeen-foot travel trailer for the trip. There were six of us: my wife and I, our two young girls, and my wife's parents. Dad always wanted to go to Alaska but never dreamed he would get an opportunity. I confess I wanted him along, because he was an excellent mechanic. Little did I know how much I would need him. I had purchased four new tires for the car and two new tires for the trailer. We carried one spare tire.

We began our adventure on July 6, 1966. Our girls had made a long paper sign, taped to the trailer, that read ALASKA OR BUST! It busted! Before we left our driveway, it flew off!

We headed west through Pennsylvania, Ohio, Indiana, and Illinois. We then turned northwest through Wisconsin, Minnesota and into Wyoming. We spent a day in Yellowstone and the Grand Tetons. Spectacular scenery! Then north through the big sky state of Montana, crossed the Canadian border into the province of Alberta and enjoyed the visits to Glacier and Banff National Parks. I rented a small boat and took the kids out on beautiful Lake Louise.

We continued west into British Columbia and on to Dawson Creek, the gateway to the famous Alaskan Highway. Upon arriving at Dawson Creek, we purchased a book called The Milepost. This book is essential before venturing onto the highway. Dawson Creek is designated Milepost 0. Each mile of the highway is marked with a numbered sign. All service stations, places to eat, and points of interest are identified with milepost numbers. It is critical that travel days are planned around these important points. It was also necessary, in case of an emergency, that we paid attention as to where we were.

The Milepost book gave us much useful information. For example, we were advised to carry at least two extra spare tires which later proved to be valuable advice. We were instructed to cover our headlights with plastic covers to minimize breakage. We kept our headlights on all day, not as much to improve visibility, as to be seen in the constant dust that was created by passing trucks. It was interesting to note how many vehicles had broken windshields. We were also advised to put duct tape around every window and door to keep out dust. All to no avail. We had fine powder dust in drawers, clothes, on our person and virtually everywhere.

Before we left Dawson Creek, we had to change the wheel bearings on the rented trailer. At this point, we felt mildly confident we were prepared to take on the challenge of the Alaskan Highway. The Alaskan Highway was a rugged road when it opened for public travel in 1949. There was not a single service station between Fort Nelson, BC, and Whitehorse, Yukon, a distance of 600 miles. It was a bit better than that in 1966. On one occasion, we desperately needed fuel. When we arrived at the planned service station, we discovered it was closed. But we simply could not venture any further without fuel. We parked our rig at the fuel pumps and there spent the night openly praying the station was not closed permanently. It wasn't! The next morning at seven the owner arrived. I took a picture of the gas pump showing the outrageous price of sixty cents per imperial gallon.

Mosquitoes were additional passengers. They were huge and very annoying. They not only stung but buzzed around your eyes and face. On a few occasions, the Milepost book would indicate a certain lake was good for fishing. I continued to try to fish but hardly ever got the line wet because of mosquitoes. One of the things we needed to get used to was 24 hours of sunlight. Around 2:00 a.m., it would get slightly dusk but then bright sunlight. I rather liked that except it made sleeping more difficult until we got adjusted.

• • • • •

The travel was necessarily slow and sometimes tedious. Flat tires were a constant problem. We had seven flat tires in this stretch. One time as I was driving, it appeared the trailer was weaving a bit. I stopped and got out and saw a flat tire on the trailer. Dad got out on the passenger side and asked if the tire on my side was flat? He announced the tire on his side was flat also. Two flats at the same time. At each service station we would have our tires repaired. Dust was also a constant problem. Often we were forced to stop when we saw other vehicles approaching, needing to wait for the dust to settle before we could proceed.

We arrived at our destination in Glennallen, Alaska, on July 16, 10 days after we began. In Glennallen there was a family of missionaries to the Athabascan Indians. I had worked with the husband at radio station WBYO in Boyertown, Pennsylvania. He moved to Glennallen to start the radio station KCAM which is still functioning well today. At one point, he tried to encourage Mildred and I and our family to join them in Alaska and help build the radio station. While I wanted to visit Alaska, I never had the desire to live there.

One special treat was the trip I took with my friend, across the Copper River to a large island, the site of the original settling of the Athabascan Indians. Women from outside the Indian tribe are not permitted on the island. It was like stepping back in time. Papoose swung on hammocks across the corner of their little huts. The one Indian woman was very proud to show me her team of sled dogs. The dogs barked constantly. Huge chunks of meat (whether moose or bear, I did not know) were sitting on the porch floor, "Food for her dogs" she said.

Moose meat and salmon were staples of the diet of our friends. Moose meat is very low in fat content, even to the point of having some value in weight loss. It is quite tasty, somewhat on the order of aged beef. Fresh salmon is a real treat. Local people also use dried salmon as a staple. It was fascinating to go with my friend to the Copper River to tend the fish wheel. This thing is ingenious! Best described as a ferris wheel that is floated out into the river secured to the shore by ropes. The current of the river forces the wheel to turn. Salmon swimming upstream, are caught in the wheel and are flipped up out of the water and into a large box on the other side of the wheel. My friend simply went to the box and pulled out as many salmon as we needed. That evening, we enjoyed fresh salmon, this one weighing twenty pounds. If more salmon were in the box than needed, they were released. I learned, at that time, Alaskan law permitted only Indians, missionary families, and other non-profit organizations, the use of the fish wheel for catching salmon.

My wife had an accident in the kitchen as she was helping to prepare dinner. She was making mashed potatoes when she got her fingers caught in the double blades of the mixer. Her fingers were so twisted in the blades, and we could not cut the blades. It was extremely painful. We took her to the nearby small hospital, (one doctor, one nurse, 8 beds). When we arrived, the only doctor on staff, was on the back porch of the hospital pulling porcupine quills out of the nose of an Indian's dog. Whatever it takes!

One final story! We had a chance to go to Valdez, Alaska. This was the town that two years earlier was so devastated by the earthquake, it was deemed to be beyond being rebuilt. The state was rebuilding the city at a whole new location, approximately five miles away. As we walked around the ruins, it was beyond my imagination. Houses, cars, debris all mixed together. The remains of a sidewalk were treacherous. But I ventured into town and saw the sink for a second floor bathroom still attached to the wall but well below my feet. As I recall the power of this earthquake registered seven on the Richter scale. The sight of Valdez is incredible!

Time came to begin our return trip! We traveled southeast again on the Alaskan Highway now being more acquainted with its varied features. I do recall coming onto a family standing along the road. Their car had gone off the road and was about two thirds submerged in water. We asked if we could help but they assured us help was on the way. The driver indicated he lost his way when a large caravan of trucks passed going in the opposite direction. On the way home, so as not to repeat our steps, we took the Trans-Canadian Highway all the way east to Ottawa. Then due south through New York to our home. We arrived home on August 12th 10,795 miles. As difficult and yet as invigorating as the trip was, I would do it again, except now the highway is paved and the adventure is softened.

• • • • •

In 1999, my wife and I, together with our good friends, Shirley and Titus Hendricks, went back to Alaska. This time via the Holland Cruise Line aboard their luxurious Ryndam. We sailed out of Bellingham, Washington, to Seward, Alaska. We took a bus to Anchorage. There we picked up a 28-foot motor home and traveled the Alaskan Highway again. Very pleasant, comfortable, but it lacked the one ingredient I craved, adventure.

●　●　●　●　●

My family and the family of Shirley and Titus Hendricks enjoyed a number of vacations together. One of those vacations was most memorable for several reasons I would like to describe.

In July 1970, we rented a 22-foot motor home planning to travel to California. There were five in the Hendricks family, Shirley and Titus and their three children, Mildred and I and our two children. Nine people in a motor home that sleeps eight. Everything went well until we reached Gary, Indiana. There the transmission of our rented motor home failed. We were marooned in downtown Gary for three days until the rental company could send another motor home. We were not only uncomfortable in our surroundings, but impatient to continue our journey. Finally, at 3:00 a.m. on the third day a replacement arrived. We were grateful but the replacement had no air conditioning. Having traveled across the desert several times, I knew air conditioning was essential.

We continued a wonderfully uneventful trip to the west coast arriving in the northwest state of Oregon which has spectacular beaches with huge rocks and high sand dunes. Titus and I, together with the five kids, enjoyed dune buggy rides over the dunes. Walking along the beach, I found a beautiful starfish lying on the sand. My knowledge of starfish was extremely limited and I assumed it was dead. I couldn't resist picking it up and putting it in the back of the motor home. Our rec' room back home had a nautical theme and this starfish would fit in nicely. More about the "wisdom" of keeping the starfish in a moment.

Days later, we found ourselves in the Chinatown section of San Francisco. Nine of us searched for a hamburger since Chinese food was unfamiliar dietary fare. No luck! I stopped at a small market and asked the Chinese clerk where he eats lunch. He told me, "Go down the street one block to a certain retail store, (not a restaurant). Next to the store was a door leading to the second floor. There is the best restaurant for all of you in Chinatown." Knowing no other alternative, we all climbed the stairs to a large open area, with attractive Oriental decor, serving Chinese food. We were greeted with a bow, and shown to a large round table for nine.

The waiter came with menus! He spoke no English and my Chinese was limited to my smile. When it became woefully apparent we were incapable of ordering anything, he took all the menus from us and motioned he would bring food. Soon, our table was filled with everything they served. There was a dish of items I recognized, some things seemed unfamiliar. We thoroughly devoured much of what they served. All of a sudden, it happened to Titus and me simultaneously. No mention of the cost. At the conclusion of the meal, the waiter handed me the bill. Carefully I peeked! $15.95 for all nine of us.

Our next destination: Disney Land. We found the campsite for motor homes, and began to back into our designated space. As soon as I got out of the motor home, I noticed a pungent odor. It was clearly unpleasant. I asked the man whose motor home was parked next to ours, what is that terrible smell. He replied, "I don't know, we didn't notice it until you moved in." As I walked to the rear of our motor home, the odor was severe. Oh boy, I knew what it was. That starfish wasn't dead when I picked it up on the beach, but it certainly was now. I improved the neighborhood by taking it four blocks up the street and depositing it in a community trash can. Good luck to that area.

One final memory of that trip. Leaving Los Angeles, and crossing the San Bernadine mountains, we began our journey east. East of Barstow, California, is the Calico Ghost Town. This town is at the west side of the Mojave Desert. How I dreaded driving for days through the desert without air conditioning. During one of my many complaining sessions, Shirley remarked cheerfully, "Maybe it will rain!" My response, "Shirley, why do you think they call it a desert? It never rains." We toured the Ghost Town. On our way to the motor home, a huge black cloud came over the area and it began to pour down rain. That rain cloud stayed with us as we traveled east across the Mojave Desert. I firmly believe the presence of rain in the desert was a direct result of my complaining!

Alaska or bust.

Typical scene on the Alaskan Highway.

Mile post 0, Dawson Creek, British Columbia.

Flat tire, one of seven.

Athabascan woman with my friend.

Salmon fishing with a fish wheel.

Shopping in the Ladies' Department?

CHAPTER 6

One of the things I did not look forward to at Christmastime was figuring out what kind of gift to get my wife. Some of my gifts I had given her in the past seemed lacking. For example, one year I bought her a machine to measure her blood pressure. That was not good! One year I thought I had come up with the perfect gift. Women love jewelry, so I couldn't go wrong. I bought her a beautiful and expensive set of earrings. How could I know she didn't have pierced ears? I even offered to pierce them but my offer was refused. This kind of information would normally have been in our pre-nup agreement but our marriage predated our pre-nup.

Just a few years after we were married, I had a brilliant idea. This time, I could not miss! I was going to surprise her and buy her a beautiful store bought dress. I should explain that my wife is a gifted seamstress. She makes wedding gowns and all of those kinds of exotic clothes, and makes practically all of her own clothes. She always looks terrific. She has saved me a bundle of money over the years, so I am in full support.

However, I enjoyed this idea because she would be shocked if I bought her a dress. She knows that I know virtually nothing about clothes. She not only buys all of my clothes, she lays out, the night before, what I am going to wear the next day. That began soon after our marriage when one morning I put on my favorite rust-colored plaid shirt, a pair of light red trousers, white belt and white shoes. I thought I looked terrific. My wife's comment when she saw it, "That outfit offends my eyes." I didn't even know that eyes could be offended. Well, that did it for me and the rest is history. I do have veto power over what she chooses for me to wear, but I have never had the nerve to use it.

I readily admit, if left alone, I would dress like a clown. I love bright colors. She claims if you are going to err, err on the side of understated, not overstated. I never knew putting on a shirt and pair of pants had such scientific ramifications. But that's why I have a closet full of five shades of beige.

So I set out for Hess's Department Store in Allentown. I inquired as to the location of the ladies' department and was directed to the second floor. I was elated at this opportunity albeit a bit nervous. I went up the escalator and walked right into the ladies' underwear department. Holy smokes, I felt like a fish flopping on the sand. I was clearly out of my element! I don't think men are permitted in this department. But before I could flee, a salesperson came over and asked if she could help me. I wanted to say, "I'm looking for the hardware department." But I knew I needed to continue if I was going to complete the mission. I replied, "Yes ma'am, I would like to buy a dress for my wife for Christmas." She said, "That's wonderful, follow me." As we were walking together, she asked me if I knew my wife's size. Oh man, I guess I should have thought of that beforehand because I had absolutely no clue. I added to my misery by saying, "She is not small, but she surely isn't large—so I guess she would be a medium."

The saleswoman smiled and then said, "No sir, I mean I would need her measurements across her chest, her waist and her hips." I said, "You mean in inches." Yes, was her reply. This whole thing was getting well beyond me. I thought to myself, if I am going to have to estimate my wife's measurements, this cannot possibly end well. I am playing with alligators. At this point, most guys would realize this was a bad idea from the start and move on. Not me! I'm too dumb to quit. I asked the saleswoman to give me a minute and I think I could come pretty close to estimating my wife's measurements. She busied herself and left me alone.

Mentally, I decided I could build a model. After all, she is about an inch shorter than me, quite trim, and so I ought to be able to estimate her measurements using myself as the subject. I thought about my chest. From the midway point in the middle of my chest to the middle of my back, I guess would be about 14 inches, so I concluded 28 inches would be right for me but for obvious reasons I'll need to add a few inches. So 32 inches for her top should be close enough. Now to the waist. I thought I remembered that my belt was 32 inches. Then obviously, my waist is larger than my chest. Therefore, I reasoned a 36-inch waist for her would be fair. Now as to the hips! Here I had no clue. Common sense tells me the hips are larger than the waist. I was fairly sure women's hips are larger than men's hips, so I plugged into the equation 40 inches for her hip measurement. I reviewed this conclusion in my mind and I was satisfied with the result.

When the salesperson reappeared, I asked if the dress could be returned if I was wrong? She assured me the dress could be returned if it had not been worn. On that basis, I proceeded. I announced my conclusion was 32-inch top, 36-inch waist and 40-inch hips. By this time, the salesperson could not stifle her laugh any longer and she said, "Sir, you have described a Christmas tree." She continued, "May I make a suggestion?" "By all means," I responded. "Does your wife have a sister or someone she is close to?" she asked. "Yes, she has a sister," I said. She asked, "Why don't you come back and bring her with you?"

I thought about that for a minute and then said, "Miss, I really do appreciate your patience with me in a chore I will never do again. "But I am going to stick with what I know best and avoid what I know nothing about. For Christmas, I'll be getting her a new set of tires for her car."

Years later I did buy my wife beautiful outfits but I took my daughter with me! Much easier!

Hunting—
The Buck Valley Episode
CHAPTER 7

I have always enjoyed the sport of hunting, especially big game, white tail deer, mule deer, elk, antelope, that sort of thing! Before I begin this story, I do need to emphasize that my inability to actually hit what I aim at is legendary, at least among my peers. It is not entirely my fault. The fact is, I have not been wired to hunt. I am right handed. In order to use the rifle scope correctly, you need to close the left eye. My problem is it is easier and more natural for me to close my right eye. If I close my right eye I can't see through the scope. Often when I try to close my left eye, my right eye closes as well. Both eyes closed while hunting is not recommended by *Field & Stream*. I tried shooting left handed but I couldn't even hit the ground if I aimed at it. I have written this for no reason other than to encourage your sympathy.

Back in the 1970s, I was instrumental in putting together a group of ten men whose idea it was to establish a hunting camp. Subsequently, we purchased a 400+ acre farm in Tioga County in Pennsylvania. The land was ideal for our purpose in that our farm was contingent to 12,000 acres of Pennsylvania forest land also available for hunting. There was a house, long abandoned, and a barn we thought was of no account. Apparently we were wrong as old barn boards were highly sought after. When we arrived one year, our entire barn had been stolen. We worked long days to make the house livable. A perfect hunting camp was formed. We named it Buck Valley. The very first year we hunted on our new property, I was fortunate enough to bag a perfect eight-point buck. That trophy hung on my wall for many years until we recently remodeled.

The following year, like the certified idiot I must be, I announced at breakfast that since I shot an eight-pointer last year, I was not coming in until I would shoot a ten-pointer. That comment received more than a little derision from the group. As we left the house around 5:00 a.m., it was beginning to snow lightly. That's good news to a hunter. Deer are more readily seen, it is more quiet to walk, and in the event of success, it makes it much easier to drag the deer home.

As the morning progressed, it began to snow much harder, becoming almost blizzard like. I saw no deer, saw no other hunters, and heard no shots all morning. I questioned my sanity in staying out in this weather. I frequently took out my compass to keep my bearings. Since we were all new to the farm, the rule, no matter where you were, just head south and you would eventually come to our road. Simple enough!

Just about the time I was going to call it quits, I was startled by a gunshot that seemed reasonably close. Instinctively, I removed the caps on my scope so I could be somewhat prepared. All of a sudden, through the huge flakes of snow, I saw a deer running at full speed. Even through the snow I could see the biggest rack on any deer I had ever seen in Pennsylvania, and he was coming right at me. As he went past, at a distance of no more than twenty to thirty feet, I raised the gun and fired. The deer stumbled and almost went down, but regained his footing and continued. When I got to the place where he was hit, there was a lot of blood, so I knew he couldn't go far. In the snow the deer was easy to track. After walking a short distance, I saw him lying down. I could not believe what I saw—a huge rack. While it was not a perfect rack of horns, and a bit irregular, I counted the points and you guessed it, ten points.

I stood in the middle of the woods in a blinding snow storm and just roared with laughter. I couldn't believe I had shot a ten-point buck just as I had promised. I took out my knife and began to field dress the animal. I tied his legs together like I always did. It made the deer easier to drag. I wrapped my drag rope around his horns. I cleaned my hands in the snow, and I was feeling mighty fine. I looked at my watch. It was 10:30 a.m. I reached into my pocket for my compass to get the direction for home, but the pocket where I carried the compass was empty. I frantically searched every pocket—but no compass. There was a bolt of absolute panic that shot through my body. Somewhere I had lost my compass. I berated myself for my foolishness and my carelessness. I reasoned, when I frequently checked my compass with my heavy gloves on, I wasn't careful enough to be sure the compass got into the pocket. I had to face the reality that I was lost. I had no idea if I was even on our property!

With no direction in mind, I started to drag the deer, hoping and praying I would come across another hunter. But inwardly I knew they were all back in their camps. I trudged on without a clue. Maybe there was a road somewhere—but nothing. The scenery was the same in every direction. I aimlessly trudged on. I checked my watch again, it was now 1:00 p.m. Still no sign of relief. By this time, the snow was getting so deep it made walking difficult. I was glad I had put a sandwich in my coat before I left the house. Common sense seemed to tell me to head down whenever I could, but I would only find a small ravine. I followed the ravine until it ended in another hill. By now it was after 3:00 p.m. I had been dragging this deer for four and one-half hours. It is going to be dark soon, and I seriously began to consider the unthinkable. I may have to spend the night. The snow may extend the daylight a bit but not very long. I checked my pocket and discovered I did have matches. I remembered reading a story in my hunting magazine of a hunter in a similar situation who burned his money in order to get a fire started. I thought of the guys back at camp. They probably wondered why I hadn't come in. They would begin to worry and ponder what to do.

Again, I looked at my watch. It was now 4:00 p.m. and starting to get really dark. At this point, it was getting difficult to walk. I stumbled over fallen trees that were snow covered. I was physically exhausted and emotionally spent. Just about the time I feared all hope of being found or of finding something or someone was gone, I thought I smelled smoke like from a fireplace. I climbed a small rise and through the huge flakes of snow I saw a light. It was on a telephone pole. There was an old aluminum house trailer out of which were coming billows of smoke. Exhausted as I was, I slid down the hill to the back of the trailer. I knocked on the door. The door opened with a blast of heat that felt really good. Standing in the doorway was the biggest mountain man I ever saw. He had a full black beard. No shirt but his wide red suspenders served him well. He was without a doubt, the best-dressed, most handsome man I had ever seen. I told him I was lost and that I had been dragging this deer since 10:30 a.m.

He looked me over carefully, commented on the nice deer and asked me where I was heading. I told him the name of the original owner of the farm we had purchased the year before. He was not familiar with the name. I began to describe the farm and he said that it must be the old abandoned farm on Mill Road. He said, "Son, as the crow flies it may not be more than a mile or so over the mountain, but you are on the north side of this mountain." On hearing that, I realized that I must have been walking in circles all day. He continued, "I strongly suggest you follow this road. This road is Painter Run. Leave your deer and your rifle with me. Walk down Painter Run until you get to a little white church. That cross road is Mill Road. Turn right and keep walking." I was more than ready to leave my deer and rifle. I followed his instructions and arrived home well after supper. I was physically and emotionally spent. The guys were as greatly relieved to see me as I was to see them. We used one of the pick-up trucks, and I retrieved my belongings.

As I relive this story, a similar sense of panic returns. Some have asked, "Why didn't I stop dragging the deer?" I thought about that a lot during that day. First, the deer wasn't that hard to drag. He slid across the snow easily. Second, I wanted to show him off, I admit. But third, I didn't want to be alone. I doubt that makes much sense to you now because it seems strange to me now too. Just having the deer with me, seemed like the thing I wanted to do.

That set of horns hangs on my wall in the garage today. I use it as a hat rack for my golf hats. It is a constant reminder to a valuable lesson I learned that day: Pin your compass to your jacket and keep your stupid mouth shut.

Australia & New Zealand
CHAPTER 8

Australia and New Zealand were two places I had always longed to visit. The opportunity presented itself in October 2006. Mildred and I were privileged to be a part of a most congenial group of fourteen, plus our host. Except for the flight that never ends, that whole experience was most memorable. I hope I can capture the essence of those two magnificent and yet totally different islands.

We left the City of Angels and a life-time later landed in Brisbane, Australia. In the process, we lost a day when we crossed the International Date Line. I couldn't figure out what happened to that day. It was just gone and no one seemed to care. I found out later it was waiting for us on our return trip. On the way home, one in our party had a birthday on the day we crossed the date line. We had a big deal celebration. The next day was the same day and he wanted another celebration. In this group, no chance.

We left Brisbane, and headed north to the city of Cairns, on the northeast coast. This area is tropical and beautiful. By wave-piercing catamaran, we sailed to the very edge of the outer Great Barrier Reef. Beautiful beyond description. The Great Barrier Reef is the only living thing visible from space. The Great

Barrier Reef is one of the living seven wonders of the world. The Reef is longer than the Great Wall of China. It is home to some of the most intricate, colorful coral in all the world. Some went snorkeling to view firsthand the magnificent coral design and the abundant marine life. It was important to those who went snorkeling to stay within the prescribed areas as there are some dangers as well. There is a box jellyfish whose sting is extremely painful and can be fatal. There is also a Blue Ringed Octopus, a golf ball-sized marine life whose sting is fatal to an adult. Those of us who did not go snorkeling viewed the Reef in a boat with glass on the lower sides, and we enjoyed the view as we slowly navigated through the crevices of the Reef.

On our return to the mainland, we were treated to a spectacular rail journey aboard the Kuranda Railway. We paid a visit to a village in the rain forest. There we had great fun riding in an amphibious army duck, literally through the dense swamp. One of the highlights was a visit to the internationally renowned Tjapukai Aboriginal Park for a great show. We were astounded at how accurately they could throw a spear and we learned, unsuccessfully, how to throw a boomerang. Let me be the first to tell you those boomerangs don't always come back. It was here that my wife attempted to adopt a koala bear.

From Cairns we headed south to the queen city of Sydney and the spectacular Sydney harbor. There we toured the world famous Sydney Opera House. Sydney is also the city where you can, by reservation, walk across the top of the super structure of the huge bridge across the harbor. There, for a substantial fee, you can risk your life. No thanks, I'll pass! There is a limit to the dumb things I'm willing to do.

We were given the opportunity to see sheep dogs perform their magic. On a sheep ranch, we observed how amazingly one dog can control a herd of sheep. He literally steered a small herd from the pasture directly to the feet of the farmer. If the farmer moved several feet, the dog guided the herd again to the feet of the farmer. That dog had all the sheep facing in the same direction as though transfixed on the farmer. We also enjoyed a sheep shearing demonstration. An experienced shearer can shear one sheep in ninety seconds.

One cannot be in Australia without wanting to see kangaroos. As we traveled along by motor coach, our guide stated that kangaroos are nocturnal and not always seen during the heat of the day. He did say we may be lucky enough to see one. He assured us, however, that we would see many other animals, including the rarest of Australian animals, the "wusaroo." We were excited at the prospect. Suddenly, the guide called out, "Quickly, on the right side of the motor coach, a wusaroo!" All of us jumped up in time to see a small kangaroo, dead on the side of the road. Yes it was a 'roo. We were had big time!

One of the highlights of our time in Australia, was the opportunity to spend an afternoon and overnight on a working sheep ranch. My wife and I along with another couple enjoyed the hospitality and the experience of this farm family. The farmer owned six thousand acres, had two thousand sheep and a large herd of beef cattle. He told us of the severe drought that Australia was experiencing. They had no appreciable rain for the last five years. He said he could only hold out his ranch for one more year without rain. He told a gut-wrenching story of a neighboring farmer who did not have the financial resources to continue to buy feed for his flock of five hundred sheep. Last year at shearing time, he called them in, sheared each one and then shot each one. You couldn't sell any sheep, or couldn't even give them away. The cost to maintain the herd exceeded the revenue from the wool. How incredibly sad!

We continued on to Melbourne. There was one experience in Melbourne I will never forget. At one point, we traveled by motor coach to Philip Island. Philip Island is the home of those adorable little koalas, mutton birds, seals and those famous fairy penguins. There we visited the Koala Conservation Center where we enjoyed a fabulous lobster dinner. Near dusk, we were invited down to the water's edge to await the arrival of the fairy penguins.

I had no clue what to expect. First, I had never heard of a fairy penguin. I did notice a sign as we entered the Center, announcing to the minute the arrival of the penguins. I thought maybe they were coming by bus! We were alerted to watch for the rippling of the water as a sign the fairy penguins were approaching. Suddenly, right on time, a huge group of penguins, about 12 to 15 inches tall, came walking out of the water. They walked across the sand to burrow into the banks to spend the night. I stood in amazement as they waddled right past me. This parade is a nightly ritual that must be seen to be appreciated. Again, my wife asked if we could take one home. In her words, they are "adorable." Of course, women like anything that is baby size.

An interesting sidebar to these fairy penguins. I read that they are monogamous! Sure enough, not more than ten feet from where I was standing (a wooden walkway above the sand was provided for viewing) a single fairy penguin stood for the longest time. This penguin would occasionally emit a sound. After quite a while, as I watched and waited, there came another penguin and the two waddled off together. Apparently the male had to wait for the female. Not much has changed, even in penguin families.

Now, it was on to New Zealand! I could hardly wait. The contrast to Australia is striking. We left Melbourne, flew across the Tasman Sea and landed in Christ Church. The next morning we traveled by motor coach through unspoiled countryside, past numerous crystal clear lakes, and magnificent green mountains loaded with sheep. We arrived in Queenstown where we enjoyed a Skyway gondola ride to the top of the world. We were treated to a dinner in the glass-enclosed restaurant. The view cannot be described. It seemed like you could see forever.

Moving on from Queenstown, we had a remarkable trip to Milford Sound and a breathtaking cruise in perfect weather. Sheer mountain walls rise from the calm waters of the Sound. I particularly was fascinated to see Mitre Peak's clear reflection in the water. It was like a spectacular painting. After our cruise, we stopped along the way at a place where you could bungee jump from a high cliff down to the water. An option was available; by adjusting the bungee cord, determined by the weight of the jumper, the limit of the descent could be inches before the jumper hit the water, or if the jumper preferred, they could be totally immersed. There was also another option. You could forget the whole bloomin' thing! I chose the latter, even though if you were 65 years or older, you could jump for free. Since my wife qualified, and it was free, I encouraged her to jump. I made a very strong argument about the money that could be saved, but alas, she turned down this once-in-a-lifetime opportunity.

• • • • •

We traveled south and that evening checked into a beautiful hotel high atop Mount Cook. I had to remember, the farther south you go, the colder it gets. During the night, it actually snowed. Another curiosity, unlike at home, here the water goes down the drain in a counterclockwise direction. Now you know!

I thought the highlight of our time in New Zealand was just the joy of riding along and enjoying the ambiance. Everything is green and lush in sharp contrast to the arid lands of Australia. Virtually everywhere we traveled, we saw sheep. All over the hillside were thousands of sheep grazing nowhere near habitation. We were told there are more sheep in New Zealand than there are people.

We returned to Christ Church, an exquisite city of beauty and charm. Christ Church is known as the cosmopolitan city, complete with the Avon River, a tree-lined canal-sized river that meanders through the city. A delightful old English tram wanders through the city providing easy access to the center of the urban activity. Relaxing walks were particularly enjoyable. One could enjoy an extended stay in this south island's largest city. Christ Church is also famous for its many rose gardens.

In Christ Church, we were given another real treat. Our traveling party was divided into small groups of two or three couples each and invited to dinner in the home of a local family. A taxi was provided for us. On the way to our assigned family, the taxi driver, knowing our host family well, told me to be sure to ask the gentlemen to show us his car. He said, "He probably won't offer if you don't ask, but you don't want to miss it." The home was situated on the side of a mountain at the edge of a huge lake with a view that defies description. After dinner, I asked our host about his car. He smiled and got up, went to a small shelf in the living room, and showed me his car. I had seen these cars before. They are exact replicas of famous cars. They are meticulous in detail—built to scale—with doors and hood that open. The model he showed us was a 1945 Mercedes SL sport model. While we were impressed, we hardly thought this was noteworthy. Our host then invited us to follow him down the stairs to his garage. There was the full-size 1945 Mercedes car he had built from scratch. He was a design engineer by trade before he retired. Every detail he designed and built using the model car to provide the scale. What was remarkable was the precision of the finished product. From the frame to the walnut dash he constructed the car by himself. He even found a 1945 Mercedes engine block which he rebuilt. The only parts he did not build were the canvas top and the leather seats. It took him two years to complete the job working every day. He was justifiably proud.

Late the next morning, we flew from Christ Church, to a most unique city, called Rotorua. We were now on the north island of New Zealand. Here we visited a thermal reserve. Rotorua is a city of hot springs, boiling mud pools, and spouting geysers. For many, this is a resort area. People come for the thermal spas believing they can be revived in these pools. There is an unmistakable odor that permeates the area. Pungent steam can arise from any little crack in the earth. A spouting geyser can shoot forth without notice or warning. The center of attraction in Rotorua was the Maori Culture Center. Legend has it that thousands of years ago, an indigenous Polynesian people known as the Maori first settled here. They are reputed to be the first humans on the island of New Zealand. Remarkable mariners, they migrated to New Zealand in giant canoes. Their fascinating culture is preserved and displayed at the Maori Center. We were treated to a performance by the Maori dancers, dressed in native costumes.

Rotorua is also an agricultural area. We visited the Agrodome for a farm type display of the multitude of various kinds of sheep. They introduced at least 15 different sheep bred for different purposes. Most noteworthy is the Merino sheep. The wool from this breed is highly sought after for it is soft, luxurious, and also expensive. As you might imagine, the women demanded we stop at a shop that sells wool products. Especially desirable are the Merino sweaters, jackets, and other clothing apparel. Much time was spent here. My only regret was that time was not the only thing spent here. Amen!

Our next morning departure was by motor coach to the most unusual Waitomo Caves. We boarded a subterranean boat for the ride into the caves. An incredible sight! The sheer blackness of the cave was illuminated by tiny lights of millions of glowworms on the ceilings of the caves. Glowworms resemble worms but they are actually insects. Up close and personal, they are usually blue-green in color, but best viewed from a distance. I actually thought glowworms were just the figment of someone's imagination and the theme for the Mills Brothers song.

We continued our journey to Auckland, the city of "sails." In the harbor, there were more sailboats than you could possibly count. Many residents have sailboats instead of cars. We made one final stop at a magnificent garden of every variety, size, and color of orchids.

Sadly, the time came to leave New Zealand. I thoroughly enjoyed Australia with all of its unique features and simply delightful people, but I would love to go back to New Zealand and spend considerable time on this truly spectacular island.

The sheer beauty of this place, from the lowlands of Rotorua in the north to the snow of Mount Cook in the south—this island comes close to paradise.

Our return flight home was wonderfully interrupted by a four-day stay on the tropical island of Fiji, in the south Pacific. Not only was our time there very enjoyable, but it broke up the long flight home. We arrived home weary, somewhat weathered, but with a million memories, probably more.

Sheep shearing.

Kangaroo, Australia's native son.

Koala bear with friends.

The amazing fairy penguins.

All in a dog's day of work.

Aborigine spear thrower known for their accuracy.

Replica of the 1945 Mercedes SL.

Golf—A Crime of Passion

CHAPTER 9

No book of mine would be complete without some reference to one of my great passions, golf. Golf is fourth on my list of 42 passions. I recently read a book written by John Feinstein called *Golf, a Good Walk Spoiled*. I don't share that view, because who in the world ever walks? Why do you think they make golf carts?

In 2001, my wife and I purchased a house just north of Orlando, Florida. The house is in a true golfing community where the golf cart is a second car. This community is known as "The Villages." There are both championship courses as well as nine-hole executive courses in the Villages. While I usually play the championship ones, my wife and I do enjoy the nine-hole courses as well.

Recently, we were playing an executive course. The first hole is a par four. We were paired with two older gentlemen who really enjoyed the game, but age had caught up with their skill or perhaps passed it. I truly enjoyed their company. At my suggestion, the two men teed off first. The first man hit a ground ball between third base and shortstop. The second golfer fared much better. His ball went northeast and left no forwarding address. Now my turn. I caught the ball squarely and it went straight down the middle of the fairway and had some significant length. As we were walking off the tee, one gentlemen said, "Wow, great shot, you must be a retired professional." I saw no reason to disillusion the man so I did not respond, but I did enjoy the illusion of being considered a "retired professional." It was my very brief moment in the sun!

My playing partners were earth moving their way up the fairway. My second shot was hit high and well but landed in the green side sand trap (bunker). As I was walking into the trap preparing to hit my third shot, the man who was impressed with my drive was shuffling his way over to stand by the edge of the trap. I imagined he wanted to learn how a "retired professional" hits a golf ball out of the sand. I swung my sand wedge but the ball hit the lip of the trap and rolled back to almost where I was standing. The older gentlemen immediately turned away with a look of disappointment and quietly said to no one, "Well, apparently not!"

I laughed for a week!

PEBBLE BEACH

Back in the late 1980s, my wife and I were vacationing in northern California. If you are any kind of a golfer, one uppermost passion in your life is to play golf at Pebble Beach. I have watched on television many professional golf matches being played there. I dreamed that someday, my time would come. This was my time. I thought I had better warn my wife ahead of time. I said, "Honey, I'm sure the greens fees will be much higher than we normally pay. But I don't care what it costs, we are going to play Pebble Beach. This could well be my only opportunity to play this famous golf course. So, I want you to prepare yourself." We arrived without a starting time, but the gentlemen in the pro shop assured us we could get on to play. Then he told me the rate! The cost at that time was Green Fees $175.00 each, to rent clubs was an additional $25.00 each. $400.00 to play one round of golf. I swallowed hard, trembled uncontrollably, and blurted out, "Well, maybe next time." For consolation, we went to the Pebble Beach snack bar for a soda. Two bucks!

THE MASTERS

In 2008, my wife and I were excited beyond description. My prayer was to someday be able to attend a practice round at the Masters Golf Tournament in Augusta, Georgia. The only way one can obtain tickets is via the lottery system. I had been sending my application in for many years but without success. Then one September day in 2007, lo and behold, I received a letter from The Masters Golf Committee informing us that we were chosen to receive two tickets to a practice round for the 2008 tournament. I can't tell you how much joy that brought to us.

To add to our delight, the 2007 Masters champion was Zach Johnson. Most professional golfers have sponsors. They wear certain clothes, and use specific clubs of their sponsor. Zach Johnson's sponsor is Aegon, an international conglomerate. Our son-in-law, Doug Mangum, is the vice-president of marketing for Aegon. Doug got me an Aegon hat and my hope was to be able to meet Zach Johnson. I knew that Zach Johnson and I would be the only two men at the Masters with Aegon hats.

The problem was that because Zach was the reigning champion, he was always in the clubhouse giving interviews and was unavailable to the fans. We were able to meet many of the golf professionals that we follow on TV, but we could not make contact with Zach Johnson. I was able to have a rather lengthy conversation with Tiger Woods. As he left the tee, he walked right past me, I said, "Good shot." He turned and said, "Thanks." That was it! While we were disappointed in our failure to meet Zach, the sheer beauty and the mystique of Augusta National will never be forgotten. Nor will all the money I left in their pro shop.

COSTA DEL SOL, SPAIN

One more golf story! This one requires a confession of sin!

A number of years ago, our good friends, Arden and Shirley Keller and my wife and I went to Spain. The Kellers knew a missionary family there. We had rented a car, and as we were driving through the countryside, we noticed many beautiful golf courses. Both Arden and I loved to play golf together. We did not bring clubs since we were not expecting to play in Europe. Down at the seaside town of Costa Del Sol, we saw the most magnificent golf course along the shore of the Mediterranean, with a breathtaking view. It was just fantastic. I couldn't stand it. I said, "Let's stop." I went into the clubhouse and inquired if the course was public or private. I found out it was semi-private, but there was no way we could play as the course was booked tight, more than full. I pleaded with the man in the clubhouse, but to no avail. But when it comes to playing golf in Costa Del Sol, I can be tenacious. I began to humble myself and beg. I said, "Is it possible there was a cancelation that you wouldn't know about?" He said, "No, all bookings go through me." "Could I go out to the starter, the man who arranges the players for the game, and ask him?" He said I could do that but offered no encouragement. I think he was just glad to get rid of me and pass this pest on to someone else. As I was leaving the pro shop, I turned and asked, "In the unlikely event we do get to play, could we rent clubs?" He replied that clubs were available for rent.

Even then I knew what I had to do. Something I had never done in my life. Some might call it bribery. I call it an investment in my emotional well-being, and I think it should be covered under Medicare. I was unfamiliar with the proper procedure, yet I didn't want to appear amateurish. Then, to make matters worse, I knew an additional sin would be required. I went out to the starter and introduced myself as a traveling American. I told him my friend and I wanted to play golf here and the man in the clubhouse sent us out to him for assignment. (Not even vaguely true.) All the time I was talking, I had taken an American $20.00 bill, folded in the palm of my hand as I shook his hand. American money was highly sought after in those days.

There we stood, holding hands! He didn't want to let go of the twenty bucks, and neither did I. After what seemed to be a minute, he said, "Do you have clubs?" I said, "Yes" (another lie) knowing we would have them eventually. He said to us both, "Pay your greens fee, get your clubs, and go over to the practice putting green and putt for a while. I'll come and get you." We wound up playing the most beautiful course in a most beautiful setting. To salve my conscience, I cut the twenty dollars out of my wife's European shopping allowance!

It must be said, I have never done such a thing before or since that day. And I'm not proud of what I did. Given the same set of circumstances, the next time, you can bet, I would sin again. Forgive me!

Morocco

CHAPTER 10

W hile we were staying in Costa Del Sol, Spain, our host asked if we would like to take the hydrofoil across the Straits of Gibraltar into Morocco. I immediately said we would love to. Had I known how the way the day was to unfold, I probably would have said, "No thank you! I have a headache."

We arrived at the dock about 5:30 a.m. for a 6:00 a.m. crossing. As soon as we arrived we were informed the hydrofoil might not go that day. It was too windy and the water was too rough. Our host remarked, "If they have a full boat, they'll go. They won't lose the revenue over such a small thing as a violent sea." Sure enough, a little after 6:00 we boarded. The watercraft sits in the water like a big boat until the engines get going. Then it raises up and skims through the water. It was incredibly rough. The hydrofoil was tossed around like a crouton in a salad. We were barely underway when lots of people began getting seasick. The farther we went, the worse it got. I would estimate 75 percent of the passengers were sick. Bathrooms remained permanently occupied. I was not affected but Mildred became quite queasy. We decided to go up on the open deck. That was a mistake of monumental proportions. People were throwing up at the rail, on the steps, and if you were downwind . . . well I don't need to elaborate. We arrived at the dock in Morocco. We literally had to help our host disembark. We laid him on the grass to recover. His face was an ugly shade of grayish green. I had never witnessed a man in that state. We learned later from his wife, he always gets sick. We really appreciated his offer to go across knowing the price he would have to pay!

The area where we landed was sealed off from the general public by a high wire fence. I realized later the necessity for the fence. We went out of the gate to a waiting bus to take us into town. Immediately, I knew it was going to be a different kind of a day. First, there were scores of people hawking their wares. Everything from small oriental rugs to daggers. There was a guard at the door of the bus with a billy club to keep hawkers off the bus. When we stopped in town, it can be most accurately described as an invasion of hawkers. Ruthless! They were skilled at cutting you off from your group much like a cowboy culls out his herd.

Immediately I made a major mistake—a mistake I would live to regret all day. A young man handed me a dagger about 12 inches long. I accepted it just as a reaction to someone handing you something. Wrong! That led him to believe I had some interest. I tried to give it back, but he wouldn't take it back. I did agree it had a beautifully carved handle, but I had zero interest in a dagger. He would let me have it for 40 American dollars. If you said no, they assumed that meant not at their price. He, along with four or five others, surrounded me. Some walking backward as we pushed along. He got right in my face, and I could count his fillings. It was unsettling. We never feared for our physical safety, but they were annoying and relentless in their pursuit. The only way we could escape, was to duck into a shop where there were guards to keep hawkers out. As soon as we left the shop, there was the same guy with the same dagger. Now he pleaded that it was painful for him to be so generous but I could have it for 30 American dollars.

I was grateful it was lunchtime. I thought, by the time we would come out of the restaurant, he would be gone. We went into a restaurant, had an interesting Moroccan meal and were "treated" to the art of belly dancing. The act of large women gyrating their mid-section left me looking forward to the guy with the dagger. An hour and a half later, sure enough there he was sitting on the curb waiting for me. At this point, he recognized he would need to change his strategy. He began to congratulate me on being the very best negotiator he had ever encountered. I had him up against the wall. Twenty dollars. I was weary of playing defense, so I decided to go on the offensive and give him my best shot. Since some part of "no" he didn't understand, I said to him, "To show you I have no interest in your dagger, I would not take it for free." I thought that would do it. He began to laugh hysterically. Apparently, that I would not take his dagger for free was one of the funniest things he had heard. Now it was time to get on the bus back to the ferry dock, this young man had been following me all day. There again was the guard with the billy club. Before I boarded, his last gasp, ten dollars. For the fiftieth time I told him I was not interested in his dagger. We got on the bus, and I took my seat. Guess what? He ran around the bus to where I was seated. The window was open about four inches. He jumped up, dropped the dagger in the window. Seven dollars. I tossed the dagger out of the window and closed it. My wife told me she bought an oriental rug from some guy. It was an act of self-defense.

The ride home was much smoother and therefore very delightful. We passed the famous Rock of Gibraltar. What a magnificent shrine. Someone said the French offered to buy the Rock of Gibraltar. If they could have purchased the Rock, they would change the name from the Rock of Gibraltar to DeGaulle Stone. (Sorry about that.) It was the end of a very different day. However, as my wife would say, "Look at it this way, you got another story." Yes, but at a very high price.

Stories Worth Remembering

CHAPTER 11

O ne of the greatest gifts given to mankind by our Creator is the ability to remember!

When we remember and recall events, or happenings, or even challenges, we have the joy of reliving those days all over again. Even the memories that at the time seemed unpleasant, take on a new life of their own. I list here some of my memories that I thoroughly enjoy reliving:

1.   I remember the birth of our two children. Oh my, I'm a father of two little girls! What in the world do fathers of girls do? Why do they make them so small? What do I do if they cry? Oh, I know, "Honey, your baby is crying." I learned quickly to lay perfectly still if they ever cried in the middle of the night.

2.   I remember back in 1969, I opened my own Real Estate Brokerage business in Quakertown, Pennsylvania. Quakertown, a wonderful town in upper Bucks County where I knew no one and no one knew me. I remember the excitement and the sheer panic that defined this event. I was most blessed to be joined by a staff of not only the finest, most qualified real estate counselors, but genuinely great people. As I remember this enterprise, what

success I have had, is due to their skill, their integrity and their friendship.

3.   I remember bagging my first deer on the first day of my first year of deer hunting on the side of a mountain in Tioga County, Pennsylvania. What a thrill! It is an unfounded rumor that I fired the gun and the deer ran into the bullet.

4.   I remember the short-term mission trips in which my wife and I were privileged to participate. As part of a team, we spent two weeks on two separate occasions in the great country of Ireland. On one such occasion, we extended our stay, rented a car and toured this magnificent island. Ireland has both beauty and charm. We served in the Czech Republic and in Austria as well.

5.   I remember my first convertible. It was a blue Chevrolet Corvair. I had several Ford Mustang convertibles later but no man forgets his first one! Man, you're king of the road!

6.   I remember attending the magnificent Rose Parade in Pasadena, California. Absolutely picture perfect. The sights, aroma, the mystique, the mechanical marvels—it was a day to remember. An opportunity was given to the public after the parade to view the floats up close and interview the builders. How fascinating was that?

7.   I remember the fun of playing in the church softball games and then taking the family to Dairy Queen for ice cream. I remember hitting a grand slam home run. Don't believe my friends when they tell you it was a ground ball just past first base and ran down the macadam for 20 minutes.

8.   I remember many years ago, one Sunday morning being stopped by our local policeman for failing to come to a full and complete stop at a stop sign. I showed him my Bible and told him

I was in a hurry to get to church. He gave me a ticket anyway. I think he was an atheist.

9.   I remember snowmobiling and tobogganing with the family at midnight on a mountain in Tioga County. We coasted down on a toboggan and were pulled back up by a snowmobile. The air was so crisp and cold, and the night so clear, you could almost touch stars. When you called out, the echo could be voice identified.

10.   I remember the founding of an enterprise in retail sales of antiques known locally as Quaker Antique Mall. My wife and I enjoyed antiques as a hobby and we thought others might share our love. We bought a building in Quakertown, refurbished it into over 100 dealer spaces and were 100 percent occupied the day we opened. We sold the business when it became more work and less fun for us. That business still enjoys good success today. It is our monument to free enterprise.

11.   I remember our first family dog, a poodle. Not good, as she developed an allergic reaction to trees. We lived on a wooded lot. I remember our last family dog. A miniature schnauzer. Very good and she rapidly became part of the family. I fully planned to leave that dog part of my estate. Tragically, she passed away one Easter morning of totally unknown causes. As some of you may have had a similar experience, there is an extended grieving process.

12.   I remember being at the last game at Connie Mack Stadium where I witnessed a crowd gone wild. They were tearing up turf, seats and anything else they could remove as mementos.

13.   I remember family hunting at my wife's brother's farm in Hamburg, Pennsylvania. We would come in for lunch and have a whole wash line full of pheasants and rabbits. My mother-in-law would prepare this monstrous meal and a great time was had by all . . . well, except by the pheasants and rabbits.

14.   I remember my next door neighbor, I called blind Mary. All day she sat with a pegboard on her lap, putting in pegs. When the board was full, she meticulously removed a peg at a time, then repeated the process. But what I remember most, she had the sweetest and most sunny disposition. She also had a sixth sense that intrigued me. She could tell who was walking past by their walk. She would call out, "Hi, Bobby." Amazing! She loved to laugh while listening to the radio. Often, I would go over and sit next to her on her porch and listen to Fibber, Magee & Molly. She also loved Amos & Andy. We would sit there and laugh and laugh together. I never heard one word of complaint. Though she was given a hardship, she wrung out of every minute all that it had. She may be the one who inspired me to enjoy laughing. I remember a real treasure!

15.   I remember visiting the land of Israel. There was something surreal realizing that "I walked today where Jesus walked." To spend an Easter Sunday morning in the Garden of Gethsemane was such an emotional experience that it cannot be described.

16.   I remember fondly an experience my wife and I had high up in the Italian Alps. On a very back country road we saw a small sign on a house, "ristorante." What a great place for lunch! We went through the front door, and turned right into a very small dining room with perhaps four or five tables. A few natives. We sat down at one of the smaller tables. There was no waitress, no menu. Out of the kitchen came a woman, I would judge in her 60s, built somewhat along the lines of a bowling ball. Her apron was tucked up under her chin. At first sight, it looked like it was covered with blood. Nope, tomato sauce. She spoke no English, I spoke no Italian. She attempted to tell us what she was serving. I attempted to tell her I had no clue. By the way, I have this tendency, when I am not understood, to increase my volume as though if I could speak English loud enough, surely she will understand. After this exercise proved futile, she motioned me to follow her into her kitchen. There were three large kettles on the

stove. She carefully lifted each lid, and I looked to see what was in there. After three choices, I pointed to one. She smiled, brought out two dishes which we promptly devoured and truly enjoyed. Time to leave, with her fingers she indicated the cost. We agreed! Delightful people like her is what makes traveling so special.

17.   I remember the time I ate a raw oyster! That was the second dumbest thing I ever did in my entire life and I don't remember the first dumbest thing. I learned it is impossible to eat a raw oyster with your eyes open. Thank goodness for a half pint of cocktail sauce or that slimy thing would never have gone down. I want to meet the first man who looked at a raw oyster and saw food. Man, I see bait!

18.   I remember being a part-time radio personality on the local FM radio station, WBYO in Boyertown, Pennsylvania. A friend of mine started the station and invited me to audition. His dream was to produce "radio with a purpose." It was great fun! When I moved on after five years, I'm pleased to report that radio survived their great loss.

19.   I remember one summer, when together with three of my friends, I flew to Silverton, Colorado. There for five days, we rented jeeps to drive the perilous, long-abandoned, gold mine roads high into the Rocky Mountains. This driving took nerves of steel as we were often within a foot or two from sheer drops of hundreds of feet. Frequently, we would need to get off and walk ahead to see if we were on the road at all. Backing and turning around was out of any equation. I remember stopping my jeep, and I had to crawl out the passenger side because there was not enough room to exit from the driver's side. When we had signed in, we had wondered why we had to sign so many forms absolving the rental company, the employees of the rental company, the State of Colorado, the Governor, and Santa Claus, from any and all injuries, death, disappointment, or marital unrest. If you literally enjoyed life on the edge, this was a great sport!

20.   I remember a vacation my family took to the U.S. Virgin Islands. Our oldest daughter was engaged to be married, and I wanted to take one last family vacation before that event. I had engaged a captain to take the four of us out to catch a sail fish. We were told to be at the dock at 6:30 a.m. While searching for my keys to our rental car, I realized they were locked in the car. I had no choice. I found a sizeable rock and threw it through the window on the driver's side. We arrived at the dock at 6:30 a.m.

Everything went well until the captain put out the lines and the lures and we began to drift slowly. My wife began to feel seasick. I had purchased a new video camera for her to take the video of my catch. About that time, the captain yelled to the first mate to get me harnessed into the chair. A sail fish had taken the lure. The first mate counted to ten and then screamed in my ear, "Set the hook." I pulled back on the rod as hard as I could, and the most beautiful sight was that sail fish "walking" across the water. It was beyond exciting. I thought what a great video this will be. After fighting that fish for twenty minutes, and then landing it, I turned to see if she got the video. It was then I learned she had been in the head throwing up for twenty minutes.

Neither she nor the camera ever saw any of it. Her report on this episode was less than enthusiastic! At first she was afraid she was going to die. Then as matters got worse, she was afraid she wasn't.

21.   The next story ended well which is the reason I enjoy remembering it. It is a lot more fun to tell than it was to experience.

One of the houses my family called home was situated on a very deep lot that had a severe slope from the road down to the rear of the property. One afternoon, I was working with my garden tractor down near the end of the property. For some unknown reason the tractor stopped, and I could not get it started again. When all of my mechanical aptitude, which consisted principally of stern verbal abuse and two frustrated kicks to the grille, were futile, I called the Lawn and Garden dealer, who promised to stop by and pick the tractor up for repair. That was the easy part, now comes the challenge—how to get the dead tractor up the steep incline and out to the road for pick up.

Sometimes I amaze myself with my native born ingenuity! I reflected on the law of physics. Out by the road was a very large oak tree about three feet in diameter. I reasoned that if I could get a long and strong rope, I could tie one end to the tractor, swing the rope around the tree using the tree as a fulcrum, tie the other end of the rope to the bumper of my car, and the tractor could be extricated without difficulty. In other words, the law of physics states, "A vehicle heading south can free another vehicle heading east using the law of diminishing returns."

I was able to locate a strong rope two hundred-feet long. I tied one end of the rope to the front of my tractor, walked up the incline, walked around the tree, and tied the other end of the rope to the rear bumper of my car, which was positioned at the tree heading in a southernly direction. Next I persuaded my reluctant wife to drive the car. I had to convince her that this plan, unlike most of my other plans, had a ninety percent chance of success. I sat down on the tractor seat, my wife got in the car and we set this plan in motion. As soon as the rope was taut, my tractor began to move. But before I had a chance to revel in my genius, I quickly realized I had failed to give my wife some critical instruction. I did not tell her how far to go, and failed to emphasize that time was not of the essence. My wife apparently thought she was heading for a yard sale, because my tractor and I began setting land speed records as we climbed the hill. I sat helpless as I saw this huge oak tree coming swiftly in my direction.

I am not a coward! It is just that I do not like the sight of blood, particularly if it appears likely the blood in question will be my own. I abandoned ship and preferred to be a spectator to this impending carnage. As I lay prostrate on the ground, I concluded that unless my wife stopped the car in time, one of three tragedies was destined to occur. First, my John Deere was to be unceremoniously introduced to a very large oak tree. Second, the borrowed rope will tear. Third, the rear bumper of my car would be lying in the middle of Mill Hill Road.

Fortunately for all concerned, my wife discovered a gadget she had not noticed previously—it is commonly called a rear view mirror. By cleverly using this device, she was able to assess the situation, and concluded that to go any farther would not only be redundant but pointless. What lesson did I learn from this experience? Just this—whoever said "All is well that ends well" is crazy.

Stories Worth Forgetting

CHAPTER 12

I t must be said that the ability to remember is a wonderful thing as long as that which is remembered is worth remembering. In my life, there have been some things I am quite willing to forget, if only I could. Remembering them in this book guarantees that I will not be forgetting them any time soon.

1.   I'm willing to forget that first full suit of clothing I got from Goldberg's Clothing Store in Souderton when I was seven years old. I was so proud to have an actual suit jacket and trousers that matched. When we came home from the store, my mother laid my suit on my bed. I couldn't wait to put the jacket on and stand in front of the mirror to see how incredibly good I looked. I noticed a tag sewed in the middle of the back of the jacket. I thought I'll save my mother the trouble, I'll just cut that off. I took a pair of scissors and cut more than the tag. I cut a two-inch-long football-shaped hole in the middle of the back of the new jacket. I seem to remember my mother overreacting. After all, I said I was sorry, doesn't that count for anything?

2.   I'm willing to forget the time I got my new car stuck in the snow in my driveway. I shoveled snow behind the rear wheels

until there was no more snow and yet I was still stuck. I decided I needed to have a push. I asked my wife to come out and help, instructing her to push from the front as I attempted to dislodge the car. After repeated attempts failed, my wife said, "Honey, why are the front wheels spinning?" How was I supposed to know I had purchased a front-wheel drive car?

3.   I'm willing to forget my attempt at cooking. Growing up with three sisters, I was persona non grata in the kitchen. But I always thought cooking could be fun. One day, I was in the grocery store with my wife when I saw a gadget perfect for me. It was a microwave egg poacher. I threw it into the shopping cart. My wife asked, "What are you going to do with that?" I replied, "I'm going to make poached eggs for myself." She responded, "I really wish you wouldn't." I said, "Why, are you afraid I'm going to burn the house down?" "Exactly," was all she said.

One day, while my wife was not home, I thought it would be a perfect time to show her how comfortable I could be in the kitchen. How hard can this cooking thing be?

The directions were simple:

(1) Open the lid. I did that.
(2) Crack open two eggs and place one on each side.
         I did that.
(3) Close the lid. I did that.
(5) Turn the poacher over. I did that.

All the egg ran out—down the front of the counter, into the open knife and fork drawer.

I had egg on my pants, on my shoes, on the floor; it was a royal mess. Before I was finished cleaning up, my wife came home. (Don't they always.) "What happened?" she asked. "Oh," I said, "that stupid egg poacher doesn't work." "Did you follow directions?" she inquired. "Of course, I always do." As soon as I said that I realized how dumb that was because I only read the instructions when all else fails. Then as wives often do, they make you look stupid. As we were reviewing the directions, I realized I had skipped "(4) Place in the microwave for one minute." Geez, I thought, this is not my fault. They should have (4) in bold type. How do they expect a guy to figure this out on his own? Ever since that time, I'm welcome in the kitchen, but by invitation only.

4.   I'm willing to forget my first colonoscopy! After my doctor described the procedure, I asked if he offered a semi-colon oscopy?

5.   I'm willing to forget a certain Christmas when I was about nine or ten. There was nothing I wanted more for Christmas than an electric train. About two weeks before Christmas, I came home from school to find a box on our porch from Sears & Roebuck. On the side of the box I read LIONEL. My heart pounded; I was getting my train for Christmas. I carried the box into the house, no one else was home. I looked at that box for a long time. No, the devil didn't make me do it, I did it on my own. I figured I would open the box, just look at the train and close it again. When I had the box open, I thought I may as well see how it worked. I cleared off the dining room table and set up the oval track. There was a section of track that had wires to be attached to the transformer. Oh, boy, what a sight. To placate my conscience, I decided to only play with the engine. I carefully placed the engine on the track, connected the wires to the transformer and plugged it in. A small red light indicated this mission was a go. There was a knob on the transformer. I turned it all the way to the right. The engine shot down the track too fast to make the curve. The engine flew off the track, off the table and down onto the hardwood floor. I stood in disbelief of what had just happened. I carefully put the engine back on the track and slowly turned the knob. Then the worst thing happened . . . Nothing! I tried to pack up the whole train set but not good! When my sisters came home they beat a confession out of me. My mother sent the train back to Sears. I never got a train until our two little girls were born. They begged for a train so I got one for them, and they allowed me to play with it.

6.   I'm willing to forget my music career. Most of my friends could either sing or play a musical instrument or both. I could do neither. Someone suggested that everybody can sing if they practice. I thought what better place to practice singing than in church. There, if you're not that good, they are very understanding and forgiving people. I soon found out that no, they're not, and no, they're not. I was singing very lustily one Sunday morning, but after the second song, the man sitting right in front of me turned and said, "Young man, there's a lot of good music inside of you." Surprised, I said, "Really?" He said, "Yes, because none came out."

        All right, so I'm not a vocalist. I'll try to learn to play the piano. It doesn't look that hard. I made arrangements to take piano lessons from a woman every Monday night at 7:00 p.m. for five dollars an hour. The first lesson, I was nervous. As we sat down together at the piano, she wanted to assess my knowledge of the piano. She asked, "Do you know where middle C is?" I said, "Well, I'm just guessing but I would say around the middle somewhere." After the third week, she determined I was an accident looking for a place to happen. She finally suggested she would pay me five dollars to stay home.

        I knew Rome wasn't built in a day, and although my musical career had a few setbacks, I determined it was not over. Later, someone suggested I consider the organ. They indicated, there is a tape you can insert that plays the hard part and you play the melody with one finger. Oh, boy, I think I found it. I bought an organ, inserted the tape and learned to play one song. It is a beautiful country western ballad called "Please Release Me, Let Me Go, Cause I Don't Love You Anymore." I played that song over and over and over again because that was all I knew. One evening, after one of my concerts, my wife came over to me and said, "Please release me, let me go, cause I don't love you anymore." Thus ending my musical career.

7.   I'm more than willing to forget the most mindless, brain-dead, idiotic, irrational, ludicrous, dim-witted, illogical decision I have ever made. This one should get the Pulitzer!

I must preface this story with the clear confession that I am critically challenged when it comes to car maintenance. Just show me where the gas cap is! To prove my point: I had to take my new car back to the dealer because I couldn't find the oil dipstick. But, come to think of it, it wouldn't matter anyway since I never check the oil. "As long as it runs," is my motto.

A number of years ago, I was planning to have my car serviced at my dealer. My warranty had expired and I saw they now charged $24.95 to service and change the oil. I decided to save the money and do it myself. After all, how hard can that be?

Despite the words of caution from my wife, I went to the Pep Boys store: I bought five quarts of oil, and the correct oil filter for my car. The clerk asked if I had a filter wrench? I said, "No." He said I would need one, so I bought one. Now, I'm all set. As I prepare to begin, I realized, oops, I need a basin to catch the oil. Off to K-Mart: Now I am set. I have the oil, the filter, a wrench and a basin. I have spent $14.50 but I'm still operating in the black! Not bad! I lay down to crawl under my car but the car is too low. I couldn't squeeze under it. Back to Pep Boys for ramps. I really didn't like the direction this operation was going, but I thought I am committed. Ramps, $29.95. Now I was operating at a loss, but I reasoned that I had the right equipment for all of the next times I change the oil. See how easy it is to rationalize? It's a man thing.

I carefully placed the ramps in front of the front tires and prepared to ride up on the ramps. But, the bottom of the front end of my car hit the ramps before the wheels could get to where they were supposed to be. My car was pushing the ramps along the driveway. I had to come up with a stop of some sort. The edge of the garage floor would work. Now, with a little more speed, and with the front end scraping a little, I drove up on the ramps. I crawled under the car, strategically placing the basin under the filter, and with my new wrench began to remove the old filter. Before I could make many turns, unexpectedly, the filter fell down into the basin, and oil was coming out, which you might think I should have expected. The problem was the oil was hot, that I hadn't thought about. The hot oil was running down my arm, and falling on the filter, thereby splashing hot oil on my face and my glasses. It completely ruined my shirt.

I had to go into the house to clean up. My wife was startled to see the mess. But she was smart enough not to say anything. I was in no mood for a discussion on the subject. I regained my composure, and replaced the old filter with the new one. I was advised by the parts clerk to be sure the filter was tight. I was all done, and in spite of everything that went wrong, I was mildly proud of my accomplishment.

I started the car. Looking under the car I could see oil was spraying all over the place. Apparently the filter wasn't tight enough. I slid (literally) under the car with my trusty wrench; a wrestler could not have made the filter any tighter. I started the car again and a fountain of oil lubricated my driveway. After much effort, all to no avail, I finally called my dealer and had my car towed into his shop. My mistake, (not that it mattered because I was not planning to save money ever again), I had failed to take the old rubber gasket out before putting the new filter in. My total "savings" looked like this:

5 quarts of oil @1.75	$ 8.75
1 filter	3.00
1 filter wrench	2.75
1 basin	2.50
1 set of ramps	29.95
1 shirt	15.00
1 towing & service charge	60.00
Total Cost of project	$121.95
Saved cost of service	24.95
Net loss	($97.00)

Is that the end of the story? Oh no, not this story! I didn't know what to do with the oil in my basin. I got a gallon jug. I filled the container and took it back to the dealer for disposal. When I arrived, the mechanics pointed their fingers and laughed. I also asked if anyone wanted to buy a set of ramps. They didn't. I sold 'em at a yard sale for ten bucks, and I threw in a filter wrench. On the wall of my dealer's service department, you may find my picture hanging there. I am their poster child for idiocy!

8.   I am also quite willing to forget the times when my influence on my children and my grandchildren was less than stellar. I recall when my grandson Kyle, was riding in the car with me and we came to a traffic light. The light was red so I stopped. When the light turned green, I proceeded whereby Kyle said, "Pop, I know what those lights mean. The red means stop, the yellow means wait, and the green means, 'Go jerk!'"

I also remember the time my grandson Ryan, who was sitting on the front seat of my car reading the computer notices; said, "Pop, what does it mean, 0 miles to empty?" It means, holy cats, we're out of gas.

9.   I'd be happy to forget my first landscaping experience. Our new house was completed, and money was at a real premium. So I decided to save money on foundation plantings, and order all shrubbery from a mail order nursery. Soon big boxes arrived containing individual plants wrapped in cellophane. There were no instructions. I carefully planted them all in strategic places around the house. After several weeks, with the exception of one plant, there was no sign of life. I waited for several more weeks, and the one plant was doing well but rigor mortis had set in on all the other plants.

Before filing a complaint with the mail order company, I asked my mother-in-law, who was experienced in planting, to look at my plants. She told me I had planted them upside down. The one plant that was doing well? I had made a mistake and planted that one correctly.

King of the African jungle.

Africa—Our Kenya Experience

CHAPTER 13

I n 1992, my wife and I had the opportunity to visit the continent of Africa. Our trip had a two-fold purpose. One of my lifelong desires was to take a photographic African safari. About this time, a couple from our church, Don and Jayne Dressler, both teachers, were spending two years as teachers at the Rift Valley Academy in Kenya, which is primarily a school for missionary children. It seemed like the opportune time to combine a visit with them and a dream of mine.

So, on April 13, 1992, after all our shots, visas, plans and preparations were completed, we were ready to depart. We had received a communiqué from the United States State Department warning us as American citizens to be constantly on guard in Kenya, as in all African countries, to the danger of going anywhere alone. Some bandit activity had been reported, so general awareness of the surroundings was imperative. We would remember these warnings over the duration of our visit.

At 9:00 p.m., we boarded a 747 British Airways jet bound for London. We arrived at 9:00 a.m. local time (4:00 a.m. our time) and spent the day in London. At 8:00 p.m. we boarded another British Airways plane for Nairobi. We arrived in Nairobi at 3:00 a.m. local time, after about an eight-hour flight. Then we went through customs which took forever plus two days. We immediately discovered we were on African time, which means "whenever."

We were relieved to find a woman holding a sign that said "NACES." She welcomed us to Nairobi, loaded our luggage (two bags out of four, the other two came later) and together with her driver took us into the city, about an hour and a half from the airport. We felt quite safe, but the thought did occur that mischief could go undetected. We checked into The Inter-Continental Hotel, and went right to bed and prepared for our busy next seven days.

At 10:00 a.m., the next morning, we met with the representative from the touring company who had planned our African trip. She was emphatic in her warnings. We were briefed on customs, laws, and other important details. In town, remove all watches, and jewelry. Purses must be strapped over the head and held under the arm. It is illegal to photograph policemen, soldiers, or prominent buildings. You are carefully observed if you carry a camera. She also told us, that in the event, that a policeman suspects you took an illegal picture, he will confiscate your camera. Negotiate and surrender only the film.

After that, my wife and I took a short stroll around the hotel without incident. We found the people very friendly. The operative word in Kenya is "jambo." It is a Swahili greeting much as we would say hello.

Around noon, Don and Jayne, together with Jayne's parents who were visiting at the same time, picked us up at the hotel. We stopped for lunch at a restaurant called The Carnivor. What a strange restaurant! It was a pavilion-type building, with open sides and long picnic-type tables. Around the outside perimeter of the building were a number of open pits with huge chunks of meat on a rotisserie. Family-style vegetables already were on the tables. We sat down, and the first waiter came by with a huge chunk of meat on a wooden plank. He inquired if I would like a piece of what he had. I asked, "What is it?" He replied,

"Zebra!" "Zebra? That's a horse, eh, no thanks," I said. The next waiter held a similar plank, and similar chunk of meat. "What are you offering?" I asked. "Wildebeeste," he answered. I asked again, "Wilde . . . what?"

Oh man, this could be a tough lunch! The third waiter . . . by now I was getting very cautious. "What is that you have?" "Wild boar" was his reply. Well, that's pork. I thought the way this is going, I better take some of this. "Yes, thank you." Not to be out done, here came waiter number four. He was serving "hartebeeste!" Good grief, I wondered if they ever heard of chicken! I found out a hartebeeste is from the antelope family. Not too bad, but I opted out. I was waiting for the next guy to say python, and I was out of there. The last guy had chicken. I was so glad to see him I was tempted to ask for a whole one! After lunch, I commented about the unusual restaurant. My wife had this response: "If you want everything like it is at home, stay home." Don't you just love it when you want some solace, and wives come up with that?

After an extended lunch, we set out for Kijabe, the location of the Rift Valley Academy, which is about an hour and a half from Nairobi. It was essential that we arrive before dark. Kenyans often leave their broken down and abandoned vehicles right in the middle of the road. Accidents are commonplace where unsuspecting motorists hit abandoned vehicles, especially old trucks. We enjoyed an evening in the living room of the Dresslers. About 9:00 p.m., Don drove us down the short distance to the home of our hostess, Marion Gibbon. It would have been an easy walk, but it was not recommended at night. We found Mrs. Gibbon to be a special lady. She was the head nurse at the hospital on the grounds of Rift Valley Academy. She was anxious for us to see the hospital. We got up at 7:00 a.m. and saw all the people waiting for Mrs. Gibbon to open the hospital. Most had walked all night, some carrying babies, all needing medical attention.

Mrs. Gibbon invited us in and gave us more of a tour of this hospital than I cared to have. We were in and out of operating rooms with patients lying on operating tables waiting for the head nurse. She was also the anesthetist. She quickly rushed to the pediatric ward, her favorite area, with us in hot pursuit. Mrs. Gibbon had only one speed—high gear—she was 66 going on 33. My wife was quite interested in this ward. It was interesting that most mothers were also in attendance, caring for the non-medical needs of their children. We spent the rest of the day walking around the Academy. The Rift Valley area of Kenya is said to be the star of Kenya for its sheer beauty. The Academy is uniquely situated for a magnificent view of the valley. Jayne had prepared a delicious surprise turkey dinner in honor of my birthday, April 16. After dinner, we retired to Mrs. Gibbon's house.

As we were settling in for the night, Mrs. Gibbon was telling us of her concern about living alone. She told us her house was robbed recently and many of her deceased husband's tools were stolen. Just like it was choreographed, all of a sudden all the lights went out! Mrs. Gibbbon went to the phone, and it too was dead. Now she, and therefore we, became quite anxious. Mrs. Gibbon told us the first thing robbers do is cut off power. Wow! She told us after the robbery, she hired a watchman who patrols outside all night but his day off is Thursday. Guess what day this was? As the man in the house, I tried to be brave, but it's hard to appear brave when you are frozen with fear.

Mrs. Gibbon lit a few candles and we sat still waiting for whatever was going to happen next. Mrs. Gibbon said, "We will just trust the Lord to protect us." After about an hour, I said, "If it was going to happen, it would have happened already. And besides, since we are trusting the Lord, that's a lot better than trusting me, I'm going to bed." I found out the next morning, soon after I went to bed, the lights came back on. Simply an example of the problem Kenya has with electrical power.

Don and Jayne took us into Nairobi to practice our shopping prowess. Many people were selling handmade crafts. Some of these people were extremely gifted. We purchased quite a few small items made of ebony. Prices were relatively inexpensive.

We enjoyed the people who were aggressive but not offensive. We returned to Rift Valley Academy in the evening.

The next day was very special. After breakfast, we piled into the van and set out for Lake Navisha, the home of the hippos. We boarded a small boat with a guide and headed out across the lake in search of the hippos. On the way, I saw my first "fish eagle," a bird much larger than our bald eagle and very graceful in flight. A real treat! We also came across a large flock of pelicans just resting on the water.

Soon we spied what we came to see. Our guide crept along quietly over the glass smooth lake to this family of hippos. We counted 15 hippos. It was a very warm day, so some of them stayed submerged for a while. The guide said they can stay under the water for several minutes. They can swim, but it appeared they were walking on the bottom. We enjoyed watching their antics for quite awhile. Just as we were leaving, one hippo was reasonably close to the boat and "yawned." What a tremendous sight to see! We returned to the lodge for lunch.

Kenya has many lakes, and after lunch we headed out for Lake Nakruma. What we saw there almost took our breath away. Pink flamingoes! Someone estimated over one million flamingoes called this lake their home. As far across the lake as you could see, beautiful pink flamingoes. The place did smell like a huge chicken ranch, but it was worth it for sure.

The following day was Easter Sunday. A wonderful Easter Sunrise service was a fitting climax to our stay at Rift Valley Academy. After lunch, we said our grateful goodbyes, and Don took us back to our hotel in Nairobi.

Africa—Kenyan Safari
CHAPTER 14

enya gives us Africa. Its wildlife, deserts, mountains, jungles, and rivers—and you see it all on a Kenyan safari. We were about to embark on a childhood dream of mine. A real safari. It was Monday, April 20, 1992.

We were scheduled to be picked up at our hotel, The Inter-Continental in Nairobi, by our Tour Company safari van at 9:00 a.m. As I looked out the front door of the hotel, a chill went up my spine as I saw a van with tiger stripes all over it. The driver came in, introduced himself and invited us to get on board. Our excitement level was well above normal. Then a surprise hit me. As we got into this van, which held about eight people, a young couple was already on board. We greeted them in English. It was obvious they did not speak English. We found out later they were from Germany and spoke only German. It had not occurred to me that we could be spending a week with people with whom we could not communicate. The driver announced we would be picking up three more people. We stopped at another hotel and an older couple got on board. They were from Belgium and spoke Flemish. One final stop and a single man from Brazil got on and he spoke only Portuguese. I thought, what a great week this is going to be.

We started out in prolonged silence. After several hours, we arrived at Amboselli National Park, and went in for lunch. Then the most amazing thing happened and I honestly believe in divine intervention. It turned out that the man from San Paulo was an attorney. He wanted desperately to learn English. The couple from Belgium stated they both spoke four languages—Flemish, German, Portuguese and English. What are the odds of that? The attorney, acting attorney-like, stated that all conversation for the week will be in English with the older couple translating. I had a week-long soapbox upon which I waxed eloquent and spouted wisdom, or maybe not.

In Amboselli National Park, our accommodations were at the Lodge. Each of the parties had a small cottage. As soon as we walked into ours, we noticed a prominent sign that stated "Don't leave the windows open or the monkeys will come in." We had noticed upon arrival, that the Lodge was overrun with small monkeys running, climbing, and making a lot of noise. There was also a large net hung over the bed to be let down to provide protection from mosquitoes.

As soon as we settled, we piled into the van for a tour across the prairie in search of all kinds of African game. The roof of the van could be opened to allow for all of us to stand for photographs. I'll never forget rounding a grove of trees and right next to the van was a giraffe. There were a number of gazelles running, and a cheetah ran away from us in a blur. We saw wildebeest, ostrich, and hartebeest everywhere. It was a thrill to just watch a herd of elephants in a parade.

As we returned to the Lodge for dinner, we were really impressed with the view of Mount Kilimanjaro. The sight of that majestic mountain could take your breath away. We all just stood there in silence drinking in the sight. After a huge buffet dinner, we retired for the night making certain we kept out unwanted visitors. We enjoyed a great night of sleep under the canopy.

I got up early the next morning and took a walk around Amboselli Lodge. I was somewhat startled to see, not more than a hundred feet from our cottage, a huge cage with a full-grown male lion. If you can imagine a perfect specimen of a lion with full mane, huge head and well-heeled body, this was the lion I saw. I stood in awe for a moment just watching him. He was lying down and looking straight ahead. I took the mandatory pictures and was just enthralled to see, up close and personal, such a beautiful and menacing animal. At breakfast, I inquired from the waiter about the lion. I wished later I hadn't asked. A British movie company was doing a documentary on the Masai people and their nomadic lifestyle. The plan was for a Masai man to kill the animal with a spear. I had difficulty forgetting that for awhile. Such a genuine waste of the magnificent creature was truly upsetting.

After breakfast, we set out again to view the animals. On several occasions, I had asked our driver about photographing Masai people. Each time he warned against it! Without permission, which they hardly ever give, taking their picture could put our whole party at significant risk. After viewing the animals in Amboselli National Park, we headed out across the prairie on a "road" that was almost impassable. The deep ruts, ravines, and mud holes bounced us around like balls in a pinball machine. We did enjoy the elephants, giraffes, and herds of wildebeests. One wild boar was especially exciting to watch although he disappeared quickly. About mid-afternoon, our driver asked me if I still wanted pictures of Masai people. He said he had contacted another driver who told him of a Masai chief who was allowing photographs for a fee. We all agreed to leave the planned route to take in this once-in-a-lifetime experience.

After an indescribable bouncing around, we came to a village of about thirty mud huts in a large circle. The driver got out and walked into the village. Shortly he reappeared with an old Masai man who was the chief. For three hundred Kenyan shillings per person, he would allow us to come in and photograph anything we wanted. Great news—three hundred shillings translated into about six American dollars per person. What we saw inside the village was well beyond our imagination. There were many tall

Masai women, each with a baby strapped to her back. If the baby cried, the woman would jump up and down to quiet the child. We learned the baby strapped to a woman's back does not necessarily mean it is her child. Their lifestyle is communal. There were no men present except the chief. The men take their cows out for grazing daily and bring them inside the circle at night. This was the worst of the worst! Cow dung was everywhere. Not only did we need to be careful but the children were playing in this filth. How these people survive is a mystery to me.

We were invited to go inside one of the huts. Only my wife and I plus one other person accepted the challenge. The hut was somewhat igloo shaped. We needed to bend at the waist to enter the low tunnel. Once in the tunnel, after a 180 degree turn, we entered the main part of the hut. It was about ten feet by ten feet, pitch-black dark, no windows, with only a small hole in the ceiling to let out the smoke from a smoldering fire on the floor. We were trying to get adjusted to the dark when I felt a hand on my wrist. Very disconcerting! I soon realized someone was sliding a bracelet over my hand. I assume one they had apparently made.

Most of the women held crafts they had made. We could bargain with each woman but before a deal could be finalized, it had to be approved by the chief. He never agreed to the agreed price. We did purchase several items mainly to show our appreciation for their hospitality. (I bought a small spear, an African shield, and a bracelet.) After all the haggling was completed, the bouncing women continuing, and the chief pushing more merchandise we waved goodbye and left one of the most astonishing experiences I have ever had. But I could not forget how incredible it was that children and adults endure in this environment of dirt and filth. Amazing!

We left the Masai village and headed for a geological oddity. In the middle of the prairie was about one thousand acres of black lava rock. How it got there no one knows. Apparently in eons past, an earthquake, a volcano, or some supernatural event occurred. Past the lava rock, the prairie resumed. We continued on to Mzina Springs for the chance to view crocodiles and hippos cavorting in the water. The spring originates fifty kilometers north, flows underground and surfaces at this crystal clear lake. We had a lot of fun here.

On to Salt Lick, a privately-owned game preserve famous for lions, tigers, cheetahs, and other animals. Salt Lick features a small lake that is lighted for night viewing. This was spectacular. The Hilton Hotel chain had tree-top rooms for our accommodations. Each room was part of a complex, high off the ground and connected to one another by bridges and walkways. There was excellent night viewing from your room or the bridges. There was a special viewing terrace near the top of the lake where they served dinner and late coffee.

The Hilton put on an elaborate buffet along the walkway. When I was in line, I saw a large shell-shaped dish that contained potato salad. Just as I approached the salad, a huge black bug, about two inches in length, flew right into the potato salad as though it was on a search and destroy mission. I was startled and motioned to the chef, the guy with the big white hat, and alerted him to the situation. Without hesitancy, he came with a spatula, dug into the salad and with a flip of the spatula over his right shoulder, over the fence went the bug with some of the potato salad attached. Needless to say, I passed on the potato salad. We were to soon find out how many bugs were attracted to the light. The floor of our room was covered with hard-shelled bugs. We slept with our shoes on!

The next morning, as we were leaving Salt Lick, our driver announced that we would be accompanied by an "escort" today. We assumed this would be someone who knew where certain animals were. We proceeded down the worst road we had yet encountered. We bounced into each other, and into the sides of the van; I kept wondering when the van would give out. The life-span of these vans must be months and not years. All of a sudden, there was a log across the road. The driver did not seem concerned, so we just sat there. Soon, a man (although he looked like a teenager) came out of the jungle carrying a large gun somewhat like an AK47. He opened the passenger door, nodded to our driver, and got in. He sat with his gun straight up between his knees. It was alarming, if not disconcerting. Our driver acknowledged the man, then got out, moved the log and we continued. What happened next was very surreal.

We continued down this very rough road, bouncing and banging, until we hit a monster of a hole that jarred our teeth. As we hit the hole, the driver's door flew open and he couldn't keep it closed. A part of the door latch had been broken in the hit. The driver announced he would need to find the missing part so he could have the latch repaired. With that, he got out, walked back up the road, and disappeared around the bend, and we were left with the man with the gun. There was stark silence. After about five minutes of uneasiness, the man with the gun got out. He said nothing to us but walked back up the road and he too disappeared around the bend. We felt a bit relieved and we resumed our conversation. What happened next aged me about twenty years.

Out of the jungle, where no human being could be expected, came a big man with an AK47. He walked toward us with a menacing look that scared all of us half to death. My wife grabbed my arm with a death grip. We all agreed to try to remain calm. We watched as the man approached. I quickly turned to see if our driver was returning; he was not. Before the man got up to our van, we saw another man coming out of the jungle. He also was carrying a gun. How quickly I remembered the warning from our State Department about marauders who were holding up and robbing tourists. I wondered, could this whole thing be a set-up between our driver and our "escort?" When the first man reached our van, he asked where the driver was. One of us (I was so scared, it may have been me) shouted, "He'll be right back." With that, both men walked back up the road. We sat stunned. What to make of this whole thing?

The driver and the "escort" finally returned. The driver found the part he needed, and temporarily tied the door shut.

The "escort" got back in the van and we proceeded down the road. We asked the driver, what was that all about? Apparently, our road was the boundary line between Tanzania and Kenya, and there were incidents where marauders came across from Tanzania and were robbing tourists on safari. The men with the guns were Kenyan soldiers stationed along the border to protect people like us. It would have helped a lot if our driver had explained all of that beforehand. I would not have lost so much of my hair and twenty years of my life.

The next day was the final day of our safari. As planned, at the end of the day, we were dropped off at a hotel in the resort city of Mombasa on the Indian Ocean. We spent two delightful days on the beach in Mombasa. We were scheduled for one more excursion. An overnight train from Mombasa to Nairobi.

About mid-day, we were picked up at our hotel by a "taxi." This car was such a wreck that I didn't think it would go another foot. The taxi driver informed me that I needed to hold the rear door shut. The man at the motel told me it was only a few minutes taxi ride to the train station. Soon I realized we were driving all over the place. A bit unnerving but it appeared the driver was looking to increase the fare. After a while, he stopped at a small brick building out of town and announced that this was the station. We didn't see any trains or tracks. He told us to go into the building which we did. We found the train on the other side of a high wall. We checked in, got our tickets and were informed by the station master that our name would be on the outside of our reserved car. We walked up and down the track, checking every name carefully. We found no name that looked like ours. There were people getting on and one car seemed to be empty. I told my wife we were getting on before we missed the train. Upon closer inspection, the name on the outside of our car was M/M Mildred, my wife's name. Apparently they put first names last.

We quickly took a tour of the train. First, we discovered there were more animals on this train than people. You don't want to know what the restroom was like. It was one size fits all. The restroom consisted of a hole in the floor about twelve inches in diameter. There was a large sign that stated "Do not use when the train is in the station." Our compartment was small but our bunk beds were comfortable. We were instructed by our friends who had taken this trip, to request first seating for dinner. There are two sittings and they do not have the facility to wash dishes. They just wipe them off. During dinner, a waiter came down the aisle serving boiled potatoes. As he got near to us, the train lurched a bit and a potato fell off onto the floor. He picked it up and put it back on the dish. I kept my eye on that potato to be sure it would not be served to either of us.

Our train ride was very enjoyable as we traveled through the African countryside and through quaint villages. We slept well and the next morning arrived in Nairobi. We were picked up at the station and taken directly to the Nairobi International Airport for our flight home. Thus ending several weeks of the most memorable and exciting times of our traveling lives.

Work?
Well, Not So Much!

CHAPTER 15

During my high school days and after graduation, I was employed at the Telford Auto Body Shop, an operation best described as the place where the animals are in full charge of the zoo. The zookeeper was a man, let's call him Perry. Ironically, that was his name. Perry was my boss, my neighbor, and truth be known, almost a father figure to me.

To describe Perry takes significant writing skills. First, all his employees would agree that he was a good employer. From that point, we would also agree that it would be the mother of all understatements to suggest that Perry was unconventional. That's why every day at Telford Auto Body was an exciting adventure. We didn't work much, but we did have fun!

Perry really enjoyed life and determined to live each day to its fullest potential. He took very little seriously—not even himself! Totally unpredictable, impulsive to the extreme, he lived for the moment. As an example, one day he announced, almost as an afterthought, "I'd like to learn to fly a plane." Now, what would the normal person do who wanted to learn to fly? Oh, I'm just guessing, but he would probably make arrangements with an instructor to take flying lessons. Well, not Perry, the first thing he did was to go out and buy an airplane. Perry spent much of his time seeking adventure. The abnormal was normal. The absurd was ordinary. The ridiculous was always worth considering. Perry was my mentor. He should get some of the blame!

I remember well in 1948 Perry ordered a new Pontiac convertible. I was a junior in high school. As usual, I reported for work after school to find Perry waiting for me. His new car was ready to be picked up and I was the cheapest labor, so I was chosen to accompany him to pick it up. We climbed into the shop pick-up and headed about 20 miles northwest to the dealer. When we arrived, I saw this beautiful car parked out in front of the dealership. Perry went in to make all the arrangements for pick up. He came out with the keys in his hand. The first thing he did was put the top down. Knowing Perry, that did not surprise me. What followed did! He handed me the keys to his new car, and he drove the truck. I was seventeen years old and a junior in high school for goodness sake, and I drove his new car before he did. I also remember coming down Route 63 toward home, and I admit to driving very slowly. Perry was tailgating me and blowing his horn. I guess he thought I was driving too slow. Man, I'm sweating bullets over this responsibility, and he's blowing the horn.

If Perry had a dominant passion, it was motor scooters. He had a number of them around the shop. Cushman scooters mostly. Eventually, the Salsbury scooter came out, which was much more sleek, so Perry switched to the newer model. Since Perry lived in Vernfield as I did, we traveled back and forth to work on the scooters. One summer day, after I had graduated, Perry announced he would like to take the scooters and travel to Niagara Falls. Scooters to Canada—unheard of! He was looking for companions, and I was eager to join him. He drafted two more guys, and the four of us set out for Canada. Perry said, "We'll plan for a week, pack light." Two shirts, the pair of pants I was wearing, one change of underwear (I'll turn them inside out on alternate days), one rain jacket. What more could I need?

Our trip north was uneventful except I recall we encountered a severe rainstorm. We huddled under a bridge for what seemed to be a month short of a lifetime. We used all roads less traveled. We had a good discussion with the police in a small town near Binghamton, New York, who thought we were disturbing the peace. His attitude seemed to indicate he was more curious than concerned. Needless to say, we attracted a lot of attention as we rode along, almost gaining celebrity status.

When we arrived at the Falls, even though the falls are best viewed from the Canadian side, Perry thought it wise not to go through customs. After being at the Falls for probably less than an hour, Perry said, "Okay guys, if you've seen it once, you've seen it. Let's go!" Typical Perry. He gets restless quickly. We began the trip home. The only thing I remember about the trip home was an accommodation one night. As you may imagine, we didn't choose the Hilton for our night's lodging. Some of the motels selected were highly suspicious. One night, in just such a motel, we spied bugs under the pillows. We sent Perry in to get our money back. If he put his mind to it, Perry could charm the whiskers off a cat. We arrived home safe and reasonably sound. But I refused to sit down for two days! That part of my anatomy was in full retreat.

What happened the very next day, is the subject of another story in this book. Suffice it to say, it very nearly cost me my life.

Every day at Telford Auto Body Shop was a new opportunity for bedlam. Living directly behind the shop in a single room "dwelling" was a true character named Jonas. To protect any of his family survivors, I will omit his last name. Jonas was probably in his mid 50s, single, semi-employed (translation, worked only when he needed the money). His favorite pastime was light and dark refreshment. He usually frequented the shop in various stages of inebriation. His lifestyle was well known in the community. Interesting to note, when Jonas was under the influence of alcohol, he was very congenial, never argumentative, and truth be told, a nice guy. However, this is not meant to be an endorsement of his choice of drink. As often as I used to see Jonas, I never saw him so inebriated that he was out of control or fall down drunk. My favorite story about Jonas is this: one day Jonas was walking down the sidewalk in town, obviously feeling no pain. Coming in the opposite direction on the same sidewalk was the pastor of a well-established church in town. As they met, the pastor greeted Jonas and said, "Jonas, drunk again?" Jonas replied, "Yea, pastor, so am I."

Jonas had no car. One day Jonas came to me and asked to borrow my car. Knowing Jonas as I did, I was very uneasy about that. I consulted Perry. Perry said, "Is he drunk?" I replied, "It seems like he is a little bit" Perry responded, "If he is drunk, he drives very carefully, I wouldn't hesitate to let him use your car. But never lend him your car if he is stone cold sober. He is a terrible driver when he is sober." After that, I used to lend him my car (he never put a scratch on it) every time he asked, because it always came back with a tank full of gas. A full tank of gas to a teenager is the gift that keeps on giving.

Not every day at the Telford Auto Body Shop was fun and games. One day ended very badly for me. It was standard operating procedure to wax and buff a car after it had been painted and before it left the shop. Buffing consisted of applying wax and then using a buffing pad that was attached to an electric handheld buffing machine. Immediately after use, we cleaned the pad for use the next time. The method of cleaning was to pour several inches of Solvex into a five-gallon bucket. Solvex is a gasoline-type product, highly combustible, that would dissolve the wax build-up. Then we would reattach the soaked pad to the buffing machine, put the pad down inside the five-gallon bucket, turn on the machine and spin dry the pad. All of us had done this procedure countless times.

One afternoon, I was going through the cleaning process. I was careful to be sure the pad was down inside the bucket before turning on the machine. To turn on the machine before it was in the bucket would spray Solvex all over the place and would bring the wrath of Perry down on you like an ax to a chicken neck. This particular time, when I turned on the machine, there was a violent explosion. I was knocked down. Solvex had splashed on to my shirt and both of my arms; I was literally on fire. It singed my eyebrows and my hair. The side of the building was also on fire. Somebody got the fire extinguisher to douse the flames to save the building. Several of the guys came to my rescue. They beat out the flames on my shirt. My chest was burned but not seriously. I brushed the fire on my right arm with my left hand. Someone had thrown a wet rag over my left arm to extinguish the flames. I was rushed to the local doctor by car. In the car I could see large pieces of black skin hanging down below my left arm. The doctor put a soft cast on my left arm. That cast remained for several weeks. Being burned was the most excruciating pain I could ever imagine. Eventually, hair started to grow back on my right arm but it was many years before my left arm felt normal. All in all, it could have been far worse!

By the way, the method of cleaning buffing pads was immediately amended!

The Day I Almost Wasn't

CHAPTER 16

July 20, 1949, as I relive that day, I realize this is the day I almost wasn't.

The very next day after our return from our 600-mile scooter trip to Niagara Falls, I went to work as usual. At the end of the work day, Perry, my boss, and I began our scooter trip home to Vernfield. We always used Mill Road, the back road from Telford to Vernfield. As you travel west on Mill Road, where Indian Creek Road intersects it, Mill Road makes a sharp curve to the right and goes up a steep hill.

As we often did, we went racing home. Perry was a good bit ahead of me. I had my head lowered to the handle bars to reduce the wind resistance. I came around the curve on Mill Road and proceeded up the hill at top speed. Because of the speed, I was taking much more than my half of the road. Whether the setting sun blinded me or something else, I do not know. I do know I never saw the car coming down the hill. We collided head on! I made contact with the car between the hood ornament and the left headlight. The damage to the car was such that, in addition to the obvious hood, fender, and headlight damage, the left front wheel was set askew, and the car needed to be towed from the scene. Later, they showed me pictures of my scooter which was severely damaged and could almost fit in a wash basket.

I was the first to leave the scene of the accident. According to eyewitnesses, I was catapulted over the roof of the car, landing on the road. I suffered a compound fracture of the femur bone, the bone between the hip and the knee on my left leg. I received multiple bruises and severe head trauma. I was unconscious and obviously in very bad shape. Perry heard the crash and came back, fearing the worse. Later I learned that Perry identified himself and took over the rescue scene. He felt they could not wait for an ambulance; he was afraid I was going to die. They flagged down a passing motorist, and I was placed on the back seat and taken to Grandview Hospital. Over the course of the next day or two, I kept going in and out of consciousness. One of the times I regained consciousness, I remember seeing my family at the foot of the bed along with a Pennsylvania State Policeman.

Thus began a six-week stay in the hospital, and a three-month rehab assignment. As it was done 60 years ago, the method used to reset my bone sounds incredibly archaic by today's standard. A metal pin was inserted through my leg above the knee. They fastened a length of small "wash line" type rope to a harness, then through a pulley arrangement fastened it to the foot of my bed. On the other end of the rope was a heavy metal weight. Periodically, they would add more weight. The theory was to gradually pull the femur bone to the point where the bone could heal at the spot where it was broken. I do recall the doctor telling me several times, that it was very likely the bone would not be fully stretched to the point where it should be. My left leg would be shorter than my right leg, and the result could be a permanent limp. The success of the treatment, would determine the severity of the limp. The only thing I worried about was whether I would be able to run again.

My six-week stay in the hospital was not that bad. I had very little pain, and I loved the nurses. (I admit to enjoying the preferential treatment and attention I was getting from them.) However, at about the point in the stretching of my femur bone exercise, when the system appeared to be working, a terrible thing happened that threatened to undo all that had been done.

For some unknown reason, in the middle of the night, the rope tore. There were those among the non-medical staff who felt the weight was too much for the thin rope. I was awakened by the crash of the weight to the floor and my body shot up toward the head of my bed. My doctor was called in right away; I remember he was furious. He ordered an immediate x-ray to determine the damage. Fortunately, the damage appeared minimal and the rope was replaced. While my left leg is still slightly shorter than my right leg, it has never caused a problem in mobility.

Additionally, about 10 years ago, I had a total right knee replacement. The surgeon noted my right leg was slightly longer than my left leg and told me with a little effort, he could make them both the same. I told him if he could make me six-foot tall, go ahead. Otherwise, I'd pass.

After being released from the hospital, my left leg was still in a solid cast for two months, and I was confined to crutches. More than anything, I wanted to be able to drive my car. My doctor got no relief from my begging about the cast until he finally removed it. At eighteen and not being mobile was the worst part of the whole affair. To be picked up and chauffeured by your friends is appreciated but embarrassing. The day the doctor removed the cast, my leg was as stiff as a log. I was told to slowly rehab the leg until it was useable. So determined was I to drive, that I lay on the sofa with my leg over the arm and persuaded my sister to bounce up and down on the leg to speed up the rehab process.

I would be remiss if I didn't recognize the hand of a merciful God at work in my life. I knew then that God must have other plans for me and for that reason, I have attempted to honor Him in all I do.

One footnote: On my first day back at the shop, Perry insisted I take a ride on his scooter. If you don't get right back on, he reasoned, you may never ride a scooter again. I did take a ride that day, but from that point on, scooters, somehow, lost their appeal. Although I continued to ride, I did so with much less enthusiasm.

The Wyoming Experience
CHAPTER 17

I was accompanied on my first hunting trip to Wyoming by three of my good friends. We would be hunting elk, and we would be doing it on horseback. That prospect had both anticipation and apprehension. Upon our arrival at this backwoods survival camp called a hunting lodge, we were oriented to our accommodations such as they were: We would be sleeping on cots in a big tent. The tent was heated by throwing chunks of wood into a 35-gallon drum. The drum had two settings: roaring or out! We met a few other hunters who had arrived at camp.

After an on-again, off-again night's sleep, where I alternated between a sleeping bag with two blankets or being naked, we had a hearty breakfast of elk steak and eggs. Next came the introduction to our week-long companions, namely our horses. I was told my horse was called Old Sam. They said Old Sam was a bit slow but very docile. Sounded good to me! I like docile. When I came out, they pointed me toward Old Sam, who was already saddled up. I wanted to get off to a good start, so I introduced myself to Old Sam. "Good morning Old Sam, how ya doin'?" Not a hint of a response. No return affection noted. Then I heard the command to "Mount up." It was then I began to realize how big this horse was. My stirrup was at my chin or at least that's the way it seemed. The idea was to put your left foot in the stirrup, grab hold of the horn on the saddle and pull yourself up. That was sheer nonsense. When I raised my leg that high, I was falling over backward and had no chance to grab the horn. Man, I'm 5' 6". Old Sam looked about 6' 10". Weren't horses supposed to kneel down so you could climb up or is that a camel? Whatever, I had no chance. I briefly thought of the way I had seen cowboys in the movies do it. They got a good running start from the rear, then jumped and at the same time put both hands on the rump of the horse, then fly into the saddle. Upon further review, I concluded that method of mounting had disaster written all over it.

What didn't help my disposition was that my three friends were sitting up on their mounts looking like the Canadian Royal Mounties, and they were laughing hysterically at my distress. I thought, okay, forget elk, I'm just going to shoot these guys. After a while, my guide got off his horse and helped me get on mine. How embarrassing was that? Worse yet, that was the practice all week. On occasion, I would try to park Old Sam on the side of a hill to neutralize my height disadvantage.

Once I was on, they called, "Move 'em out." Seemed clear enough to me and every other horse except Old Sam. Maybe his native tongue was Spanish. In any event, Old Sam didn't move a muscle. We just stood there. Since we had just met, I didn't want to apply any physical encouragement, so I tried to appeal to his better nature. "Come on Old Sam, did you notice we are all alone?" Finally, he began to twitch. It wasn't much, but it was more than I had. He slowly began to walk. Now, Old Sam's gait could not be confused with the speed of light. It was more like the speed of light years. By the time Old Sam got into the spirit of the occasion, the other horses were well ahead. I soon learned that riding Old Sam was like playing "fetch" with a turtle. His pattern of being maddeningly slow continued all day. We were always dead last. When you are last in a train of horses, the view never changes.

Once we reached the mountain area chosen for hunting that day, we split into two groups, each with two hunters and one guide. My hunting partner was my good friend Mel. We hunted all day on Monday without seeing any elk. We were assured we would see plenty of elk before the week was out. We didn't see any elk on Tuesday either. On Wednesday and on Thursday, we did see some doe elk, but our license was for bull elk only. Basically, we just had long, daily horseback rides. Old Sam's disposition was beginning to match mine. On Friday morning our guide told us he knew we came for bull elk, and we rode the high ranges to find them albeit without success. Friday, he said, "We will drop down one range to where we are more likely to find smaller elk, but we could get lucky and find some bulls." Then he told me he needed to find a doe elk for his family's meat supply for the winter. The reason he didn't shoot during the week was that he didn't want to scare off any bulls that might be in the area.

We hunted the lower range all day Friday without a glimpse of any elk. About 4:00, as the sun was beginning to set behind the mountain, we spotted several doe elk across the valley on a high ridge. We began to track them until the guide felt he had a reasonable shot. He got off his horse, rested his elbow on his knee and shot. One animal fell and quickly got up again and disappeared over the ridge. Our guide said, "Bob, she's been hit, I must go after that animal. Here's what you need to do. Listen carefully. Just sit still, don't touch the reins or attempt to steer Old Sam. Hold on to the horn of the saddle, and Old Sam will take you down the mountain and back to camp. Mel's horse will follow Old Sam." With that, he jumped on his horse and was gone.

For a brief moment, I wondered what had just happened. Here we were on the top of a mountain in Wyoming, with an old horse who was reluctant to move. But I decided our options were limited. So I gently moved the reins to the top of his neck, and grabbed hold of the horn with both hands. (I figured I didn't need them folded for praying anyway.) Again Old Sam exercised the one trait he did well, standing motionless. Then inspiration hit him and he began to move. What really troubled me is that he started to walk in the direction he was heading. I thought, what are the chances that he just happened to be headed toward home. I would have rather seen him walk in a few circles with his ears in the air like antennae until he sensed the right course. We started out in the semi-darkness but at his pace, we found ourselves in the blackest of black woods very soon—no stars, no moon, no nothing. I literally could not see the head of my own horse. I was being chaffed by trees as Old Sam was squeezing his way through the woods. A cynical rider might suspect Old Sam of trying to get rid of me. Not a chance, I had a death grip on his neck. I called out to Mel, "Are you still following me?" "Yea, but I can't see you, I think we're just following the sound," was his response.

What was quite clear to me was that we were not on any kind of recognized trail. We were just walking through the woods. We walked for well over an hour, probably closer to two hours. Suddenly, Old Sam's head went down, and I was almost catapulted right over his head. My feet flew out of the stirrups, and in desperation I wrapped both arms around Old Sam's neck, dug my heels into his side and just hung on. I soon realized we were going down a steep bank. About the same time, I heard a yell from behind. It was Mel. "Holy cats," he said, "I nearly fell off. Where are we?" I replied, "I have no idea, are you alright?" Assuring me he was okay, we proceeded on. Now I could tell we were walking through a stream. The first positive sign! When we left camp in the morning, our guide said we would be crossing a stream. Old Sam was going to want to drink; don't let him drink. Just as quickly, Old Sam began to leap frog his way up the opposing bank. I was prepared for this move; I figured what goes down must come up. Soon after the stream, I could see the lights of our camp in the distance. I'm telling you I could have kissed Old Sam. Well, on reflection, not so much!

Although supper was long past, the cook prepared a good meal for Mel and me, and we went to bed. The next morning, after breakfast, as we were preparing to leave, our guide came to my table and said, "Bob, I'm really glad to see you. Old Sam had never been asked to do that before."

Westward Ho Ho Ho

CHAPTER 18

Bruce Musselman, one of my best friends, grew up in Vernfield with me. While Bruce is his given name, I have always called him Pete. Pete wrote a great book entitled *Old Vernfield Remembered*. His book chronicles much of what I remember about old Vernfield. While everybody has to be from somewhere, I'm proud to call Vernfield my real home.

Pete and I spent a lot of time doing things together like sharing a bottle of olives. I ate the olives, and Pete drank the juice. Pete built a sailboat, and I watched as the poor thing sank on its maiden voyage. We worked together each summer at the local postcard factory. To this day, I believe our calling was to build patience, tolerance, and character in our boss. Pete and I were also business partners. We bought a market route where we sold farm products to the city folk in Philadelphia. It was a blast—which also quite accurately described the sounds our delivery truck made. The business venture had only one small problem: It is commonly known as profit, except that we didn't have any. The only way we escaped the ignominy of bankruptcy was to persuade a friend that this venture would greatly enrich his life. I wonder whatever happened to him? Probably living the good life in the Bahamas.

My mother had a brother and a sister living in southern California. I had always sought adventure and had an insatiable desire to travel. The summer of 1950, one year after graduating from high school, I felt the urge to go to California. I didn't particularly want to go alone so I persuaded Pete to join me. What followed next is so incredibly stupid that as I am typing this, I am doing so with the shades drawn and the lights out to avoid embarrassment.

I felt as two young guys, we needed a certain kind of car for a venture with so much promise. I was employed at an auto body shop after school and summers and so I had access to people who could help. I paid $35.00 for a 1935 Ford Roadster at a junkyard. The man who owned the junkyard recommended this car. He told me it ran good so I saw no need to have it inspected mechanically. Besides, I reasoned, what more could go wrong with a car already in the junkyard. This convertible even had a rumble seat. Wow, perfect! This would be a great attraction to all the pretty girls we would be bound to meet at the corner of Hollywood & Vine.

Only one thing I thought was needed—a complete paint job. Even though both Pete and I were extremely handsome and totally irresistible, I figured we had better play it safe and have an attractive car. I feared that no girl would give a second look at a black car even if it was a convertible with a rumble seat. So I painted the car. Are you ready for this? The body was robin egg blue. The fenders were canary yellow. Man, we didn't have a car, we had a bird sanctuary!

We were ready! Bring it on and don't hold us back!

I'll never forget that Sunday afternoon, the day of our departure. My mother made me go to church in the morning hoping for some divine intervention to this mindless enterprise. The car was packed with not much and parked out in front of our house in Vernfield. The news spread quickly that we were actually going to do this. A great crowd gathered, including every one of the 22 residents of Vernfield. There were people we didn't even know stopping to be part of this gala affair. All of our friends together with our relatives were assembled. Later, Pete and I discussed the opportunity we missed in not selling hot dogs to help finance the trip. It was clearly a carnival atmosphere. Everybody was so excited, well, not everybody. My mom and Pete's mom were holding on to each other, and both were crying.

Finally, all the hugs and kisses were over, and it was time to leave. We both got in and made one final wave and bon voyage. One small problem! The car wouldn't start; the battery was dead. The last sight our mothers had of their sons, was a bunch of friends pushing this car down Route 63 on our way to California.

We were not encumbered with a lot of forethought or advanced preparation. We took a limited amount of clothes (probably expecting to wear the same thing every day). We took a complete tool box, although neither of us knew anything about mechanical repair. We also took a butane cook stove and a small tent planning to stop along the road to eat and sleep. That plan would have been more effective had we first checked to see if either of us knew anything about cooking or tenting. Those two items remained unused and became accessories to the car.

In order to get to California before it closed, and all the pretty girls grew too old, we would drive through the night, a new experience for both of us. At one point in the wee hours of the morning, Pete was sleeping and I was sleepy! I clearly recall seeing a sign that read "construction zone ahead, stay alert." The next thing I remember is a loud "bang" and seeing an orange, empty fifty-gallon drum shooting off at a forty-five degree angle, bound for who knows where. I quickly stopped to determine if there was any damage to my cream puff. Seeing none, and assuming the construction company would eventually find their drum, we decided this through-the-night strategy may not be in the best interest of the car. You may wonder, after such an ignominious beginning to the adventure, did we ever get to California.

We got as far as Tyler, Texas. There that poor thing just didn't want to go another mile. I was smart enough to have taken the car title along for just such an occasion. There was a used car lot down the street, and I was able to persuade our reluctant chariot to go a few more blocks. In front of the lot, my robin egg blue cream puff coughed, choked, and gasped for air but to no avail. It died before our very eyes. After the owner of the used car lot was convinced I had not stolen the car, he offered $75.00. Being sentimental over a car only goes so far. Not nearly as far as $75.00 so I quickly said SOLD. But now what?

I confess that geography was not my strong suit in school. Truth be known, I didn't have any strong suits in school except tennis. I always thought Texas was very close to California. We could take a train for this short hop. We took a taxi to the Tyler train station. It was there we learned that Texas is only halfway to California. Well, after all we had put into this venture, we couldn't go home, I mean, we just couldn't. Pete had an idea. He announced that he had relatives in Florida he hadn't seen in many years, but it was worth a shot. Besides, there were plenty of pretty girls in Florida too. Hearing that, I was easily persuaded!

We decided he should call his relative and maybe we could board with them for awhile, get jobs, go to the beach, and the whole plan could be salvaged. Pete got their phone number from information and called them. I will never forget the conversation from this side of the phone. It went like this: "Hello Lois, this is Bruce. No, Bruce Musselman, no, I'm Melvin's son. No, I'm your cousin from Pennsylvania. Yea, that's right, it has been a very long time. Where am I? Right now my friend and I are in Tyler, Texas. That's a very long story. I was wondering if we could come and visit with you for a little while." Why she said yes is anybody's guess. We spent the $75.00 on two tickets on the overnight east-bound train to Hollywood, Florida. We lived with them for about six months, both of us got jobs and then both of us got homesick. We boarded a north-bound Greyhound that took us back to Vernfield, not much wiser but with great stories to tell.

Switzerland—
Mountains Declare His Glory
CHAPTER 19

In 1975, I purchased a car here in America but actually took delivery in Germany. In those days, the value of the American dollar was so high that one could take delivery in Germany and save enough money to cover the round-trip airfare and the two-week stay in Europe.

The two weeks afforded us the opportunity to tour parts of Europe like Germany, France, Austria, Italy, and most especially Switzerland. In my biased view, there is no more beautiful scene on earth than the Swiss Alps. Among the many pleasures we found in Switzerland, I want to tell you of a great experience that was remarkable if not a bit nutty.

For a number of years, as a hobby, my wife and I collected bells. All kinds and sizes of bells, often found in gift or souvenir shops all over the world. One day I decided to take a map of Switzerland and follow a road that climbed the mountain to a dead end. I just wanted to see how far we could get. On this road, with very little traffic, we were impressed with the beautiful sounds of cowbells. We would stop along the road and turn down the windows to listen to some of the most beautiful music as cows grazing all over the mountain sang their individual tunes.

As we neared the top of the mountain, I stopped to observe an old man tending his few cows beside a very small but picturesque barn. He was about 100 feet down from the road. I was enjoying the scene when all of a sudden, I was struck with a most remarkable idea. I would like to buy a cowbell taken directly from a Swiss cow. Even my wife, who is quite used to hair-brained schemes of mine, thought this idea was absurd. But I thought it was worth a try!

My daughter, Patti, and I got out of the car and ventured very slowly down toward the farmer, his cows and his barn. (I had my daughter video the event.) So as not to frighten the farmer (he was holding a pitchfork), I was waving my arm. As I approached, he didn't move. He just stared at me. I could see a man probably in his 70s or so, his skin brown and wrinkled by the wind. I reached out to shake his hand; he didn't move. I said, "Hello." No response! I asked him if he spoke English, although I assumed that was a dumb question; he offered nothing. I was not doing too well in my pursuit of a cowbell from a cow. I was not sure what my next course of action should be. So, I opted for a direct approach. There was a small cow standing near me that never moved, just stood there chewing her cud and in no way was she intimidated by me. I slowly walked over to the cow, pointed to the bell and showed the farmer my roll of Swiss francs. What the farmer was thinking, I don't know, because he made no sign of understanding. His facial expression never changed. I pressed on.

The strap that held the bell was about three inches wide and very stiff with a buckle that was difficult to remove. What was amazing to me was that the cow never moved; she just stood there. After a struggle to remove the bell, as the strap was old, hard leather and the buckle was rusty, I finally succeeded in removing the bell. The farmer watched without comment, without change in his expression or movement of any kind. He just held on to his pitchfork. I held the bell in my hand and again showed him my money. I peeled off a Swiss franc note. He finally responded by shaking his head no. I repeated the peeling until he surprised me by reaching out his hand and taking the money I had peeled off. I stood there for a brief moment to see if there would be any more response. There was the same stoic expression. As I was leaving with the bell, I reached out to shake his hand, and this time he shook my hand but there was still no smile or change in his facial expression. I waved goodbye but he had no response. The entire transaction was completed without one word from him. I had no time to calculate what I had paid for that bell but it was worth every cent. Today, that bell hangs on the wall in my office and I still enjoy the memory.

I could not help but wonder if he thought, another crazy American. I hoped I had not done irreparable damage to our international relations. Later on a ferry crossing a lake, I met an American who had been living in Switzerland for many years. I told him the story. He laughed when I told him how many Swiss francs I had given the farmer for my bell. He said I could have bought the cow for that sum.

One final note on this story. We left the farmer and continued to climb on this narrow road until we came to a gate across the road. I turned the car around, and as we passed the barn of my farmer friend, I saw no sign of him. When we reached the bottom of the mountain and entered a small rural town, my wife spotted our farmer friend, just getting off his bicycle and going into the town bank. At least my money found a good home.

GLACIER EXPRESS

In 1993 my wife and I, together with our good friends, Arden and Shirley Keller, were able to do something I had long desired to do, take a ride on the renowned Glacier Express. This famous mountain railway travels from St. Moritz to Zermatt, at the foot of the famous Matterhorn. It is a seven and one-half hour railway journey across 291 bridges, through 91 tunnels and across the Oberalp Pass. This is a panoramic trip through the very heart of Switzerland. The Glacier Express travels a picture-perfect route through Alpine valleys to vistas that leave you speechless. It winds its way at a slow speed where one can capture in the heart what the eye can behold.

Passengers experience an engineering marvel as the train disappears inside a mountain. A passenger can sense in the dark, the circuitous spiral until the train bursts forth into the sunlight at a higher elevation. The glass observation cars allow a 180-degree view of this masterpiece of God's creativity. The Alpine villages are quaint and have Norman Rockwell type settings. Then finally, at the end of the seven and one-half hour journey, you disembark into the shadows of the majestic Matterhorn in the village of Zermatt. If there is a day spent anywhere in travel to rival the Glacier Express, I have not yet found it!

Remnants of a scooter.

Old Sam. My Wyoming experience.

Swiss cowbell.

Jeep in Rocky Mountain High.

My Irish Driving Adventure

CHAPTER 20

My wife and I wanted to spend some time in the beautiful country of Ireland. We flew into Dublin and at the airport I rented a car. What followed was a whole litany of challenges.

First, the car I rented was an Opal. The girl behind the counter was very courteous, and when the paperwork was completed, she handed me the keys and said, "Good luck and enjoy your time in Ireland." I found the assigned car and began the transition to European driving.

The steering wheel is on the right (wrong) side. This car was not automatic drive but stick shift. I would need to shift with my left hand which was awkward. I checked all the vital signs, 1, 2, 3, and R. I started the car, put the gear shift in 1, and slowly eased out of my parking space. The very first thing out of the gate to the street was a round-about; we call them traffic circles. First, in America, we go counterclockwise in traffic circles, the Irish hadn't learned that so they go clockwise. After spending most of the morning going in circles trying to get to the chosen road, we were on the straight away. In a relatively short time you can get adjusted to driving on the left side of the road. But there is still heart palpitation when you see traffic coming toward you, as it seems as though they are on your side of the road.

I was beginning to feel comfortable when I was told by my wife, my traffic engineer, I had missed the road we wanted. No problem. It's called a U-turn. Unfortunately I didn't choose the best place to turn around plus with the combined very short turning radius of the Opal, I could not make the U-turn in one turn. I needed to back up. I could not get the gear shift into that "R" spot. I pushed down, pulled up, twisted, bent over, but I could not figure out how to find reverse. Now I was in the middle of the road. Time for decisive action. In front of me was a bank. I had no choice except to go for it. I went forward, up the bank with the car at a perilous angle. We came bouncing down to the road. I had grass, mud, and debris from the 1700s wedged under the car.

Assuming I would need sometime, during our stay, the ability to back up, I figured I had better find reverse. After relaxed searching, I found a very small lever under the knob of the gear shift. When you lift that lever with your finger, you are able pull up and move the gear shift into reverse.

One thing I failed to do before going to Europe was to learn international signs. In one city, I saw a wide entrance to a cement street. I made my turn and had not gone very far until I found people walking in the middle of the street. I tooted my horn. They gave me quizzical looks and then moved over to let me pass. I needed to do this several times. I also noticed the street was getting more and more narrow, and it was getting harder for the people to get out of my way. The quizzical looks became less quizzical and more confrontational. Then I saw it. A long flight of steps leading up to a huge government building. I quickly assessed the situation. I didn't think even in Ireland, there should be steps in the street. I had two options. I could race the engine and attempt to scale the steps. Or I could back all the way down past all those tooted people. I chose the latter option but to avoid total embarrassment I put on a hat and dark glasses, hoping nobody would recognize me.

• • • • •

My major blunder happened in the city of Tralee, famous for their exquisite rose garden and the world renowned Rose of Tralee. Tralee was founded around the 1500's and I quickly learned that most of their streets are just wide enough for one car and virtually all of the streets are one way. There are very few sidewalks simply because there is no room. Buildings are built to the street's edge. Pedestrians walk in the street. Travel in the city is at a snail's pace because your car follows people down the street like you are all in a slow moving parade.

We wanted to see the rose garden and found it quickly enough but could not find a place to park. We finally located one spot several blocks from the garden. Because it was overcast and misting, I decided not to take my camera; we would just enjoy the walk through the magnificent rows of roses. Then, much to my surprise, the skies cleared and the sun came out beautifully. I told Mildred to sit by the garden gate, and I would walk to the car and retrieve my camera. As I was on my way, there at the gate, were two empty parking spaces. What good fortune! When I got to my car, I decided to drive back and park at one of those empty spaces. I left my parking space, made my first right turn, made the next right turn, and then when I was preparing to make the third right turn to get to the garden, I realized that street was a one-way street but in the wrong direction. I was forced to make a left turn. What made it more frustrating, I could see those two empty parking spaces but I could not get to them. I began making lefts and rights until it was painfully obvious I was lost. Very soon, I recognized the road I was traveling was the same road we used to enter the city. But I was leaving town. I made a U-turn to get back but still had no clue where I was going. It had now been 20 minutes since I had left my wife at the gate.

I wandered around the city making right and left turns, becoming more and more confused and with a growing frustration at my pace, and the futility of this exercise. I was berating myself for moving the car. Why didn't I leave well enough alone? Couldn't we walk a few blocks? I entered one street; people were plastered against the walls of the building. I was always concerned about driving over their toes. There was a man who I thought could perhaps help me. He was after all, right at my window. Unfortunately, he spoke Gaelic. I am not fluid in Gaelic but he seemed to understand my question and began waving his arms in a circle, indicating that I needed to make several turns.

By now, the angst had built to a crescendo. I knew Mildred would be worried; it had been almost 45 minutes since I left her. I decided to follow what I thought the gentleman had in mind. Before I realized where I was, I found myself on the same street with the same man plastered against the same building. I tried to avoid eye contact. He seemed to know what I meant so I must be close to the garden. I decided to repeat the instructions with one less turn. Then I saw on the side street the statue that stands at the entrance to the garden. As I'm sure you gathered, by now, both spaces were gone. Fate has a warped sense of humor. The only parking space I could find was the one I left 45 minutes earlier.

As I walked back toward the gate, Mildred came running toward me as she had seen me driving by. What would be an appropriate comment for me to make on such an occasion? I said, "Honey, what happened to you?" The short leash she put around my neck was not all that uncomfortable.

A fitting and most impressive climax to our time in this beautiful country was the evening my wife and I spent on the shore of Galway Bay. We were seated in a small Irish café overlooking the bay, with perfect weather. Almost magically, we watched the moon rise over Galway and watched the sun go down on Galway Bay. Amen!

Okay, So I'm Not a Geek

CHAPTER 21

I have had a hate and hate affair with my computer for many years. It all started with a cute little desktop named Dell. For some reason, Dell hated me from the very beginning, and I remain at a loss to understand why. I treated her with the utmost respect. I knew from the start she was much smarter than I was, although I didn't appreciate the way she flaunted her superiority. But truth be known, I didn't find Dell very appealing either. I found her to be obstinate, always insisting on her way. She was totally devoid of feeling, narrow minded and absolutely incapable of compromise. No give and take, with her it is all take. I can easily understand why "windows" is such an integral part of Dell because I wanted to throw her out the window about three times a day!

Along about the mid to late 1970s, I could see the computer age charging into my world like a run-away express train and I needed to get on board or get run over. So the question was, what is the best way to learn to manage this computer age and specifically how to use and benefit from these mysterious computers themselves.

I discovered what appeared to be the perfect answer. An ad in our local paper announced the start of an evening school, where a novice could learn all they needed to know to navigate through the complex world of computing. I called the number and spoke to the person in charge. Three hours per night, three nights per week, for six weeks. 54 hours of intensive one-on-one training. $400. Fair enough! One very important issue had to be understood before I could sign up. The instructor must understand that I know less about computing than the person who knows nothing. Is this the class for an idiot? I was assured this class is entry level, and perfect since there will be only three students. On that basis I signed, I paid, and I planned, for that first encounter.

On that first night, I arrived early, found the designated room and walked in to find the other two students already there. As soon as I entered the room, this man rushed over like I had just been freed from 20 years of captivity, in the jungles of Ecuador. He was so overjoyed to see me it was difficult for him to express his delight. I couldn't help but wonder if the other guys were appreciated this much. Allow me to describe this instructor:

First, he was a soprano! When he spoke, the words came out like in a muted scream. He was wearing large, round, wire-rimmed glasses that seemed like stage props. Being in the people business for many years, I developed a first impression theory, which was often quite accurate. I concluded this guy could not distinguish a football from a hockey stick and I would bet his favorite food was quiche.

Now, to the first order of business. We must introduce ourselves. I announced my name, that I was a Realtor by profession, and was interested in learning the computing phenomena for business and personal use. The second student, much younger than I announced his name and said he was employed by a company that designs software. Since I was unfamiliar with the word software, I assumed he worked for a company that designs women's clothing or some other soft wear. The third student, middle aged, announced his name and told us he was a doctor by profession. He also said he had built a primitive computer using some plans from *Popular Mechanics*. He began an exchange with the instructor in language I could not comprehend. He kept mentioning hardware. I assumed he was referring to Home Depot where he bought the parts for his computer. We were officially welcomed into the group.

The instructor spent the rest of that first hour dramatically telling us, that from this evening on, our lives would be inexorably altered as a result of our being present in this class. The computer would change our lives forever. Eye hath not seen nor has ear heard all that is in store for us, as soon as we learn to use the unlimited resources of this new world. I expected he would soon move us to a rocket ship he had parked outside. I kept wondering if my wife knew I was moving to another planet. End of the first hour! I knew nothing more about computers than when I arrived. The best part of the evening so far had been the bathroom break.

After a 10-minute break, with coffee and doughnuts (at least the whole evening wouldn't be shot), we moved to the computers. My computer said McIntosh: I thought what a strange name for a computer. Now the learning would begin. Well, maybe not yet. The instructor began to explain just how a computer works. He began using terminology I had never heard. He talked about his hard drive. I wondered if he had gotten lost on his way to class. He mentioned a keyboard. Finally, an item I related to. (I had taken two years of typing in high school.) Then he held up a small thing he called a mouse. What in this world was this man talking about? Then came his emphasizing the need for a monitor (oh, my goodness, I knew what hall monitors did in school), we would be using a modem, he referred to a CPU and a URL. Finally, he mentioned booting and I couldn't agree more. Let's boot this nonsense out and get to learning. I remained amazingly patient but I only have so much of that stuff. By this time, my nerves were on the outside of my shirt. I told the instructor, I didn't care if there were three blind mice on a treadmill inside, I wanted to learn to do something constructive. He assured me that was next.

I sure hoped so!

First, he said, "Let's do an exercise." From what I had learned so far, I hoped he wouldn't say let's begin by doing deep knee bends. He put some instruction on the board that we were to follow on our own computer. I was waiting for the signal to turn the computer on when I noticed the other two students were typing away and appeared to be having a good time. I said, "Hey, hello, I'm over here in the ditch." The instructor came over and told me to turn on my computer. Okay, where is the switch? He turned it on. He began to write more instructions on the blackboard. After 4.5 seconds, the other "students" were sitting back with arms folded. Meanwhile, I began to type for five seconds, then an ear-piercing "beep." What was that? Each time I hit a wrong key, there was this irritating "beep." I soon learned that "beep" was to define my entire evening. I complained to the instructor about his comment regarding entry level learning. He said I was not giving it enough time and that computing is a complex study. He did acknowledge his surprise at the advanced state of the other students, and promised to be more one on one with me.

I went back two more sessions, and I felt the other two students were being held back by my total ineptness. I was getting way too frustrated, and the other guys were getting way too fat on doughnuts. After one week of disappointment, and total failure, I resigned. I suspect the other two students concluded it was the only thing I did right in the entire week.

In the past 30+ years, I have advanced a bit. I have out-lived four desktops and now I'm romancing a laptop named Toshiba. Why I have a laptop when I don't even have a lap remains a mystery. I still get frustrated, and my strong desire to smash this thing is an everyday occurrence. As a matter of fact, today has not been a good day. Things are rapidly coming to a head! I said, "Toshiba, we need to talk. I am very unhappy in our relationship! You continue to do things that irritate me. For example, what did you do with my desktop icons? All of a sudden they're gone and I want them back. I told you time after time, don't send my e-mails until I finish the letter. I am getting tired of apologizing for e-mails sent mid-sentence. And another thing: stop those 'beeps' and 'snorts' you make, those noises really annoy me. And while I'm at it, when I use spellcheck, stop responding with: no spelling suggestions.

"Toshiba, I want this relationship to work. But I really am at my wits' end. I can't live with you and I can't live without you. I have thought of counseling but I knew you would never change. Many times I sought counseling on my own but each time the counselor seemed to take your side. Why is everything my fault? I don't know if you want this union to work or not but I will tell you this, if you keep acting up and remain arrogant, I can buy another laptop just like you, and you'll end up single forever, with no chance for a long-term relationship. Think about that loneliness before you 'beep' me again."

Hot Air Balloon Saga

CHAPTER 22

R ecently, there was a great movie starring Jack Nicholson and Morgan Freeman entitled "The Bucket List." It was the story of two old men who didn't expect to live very long. Each had made a list of what they really wanted to do before they "kicked the bucket."

From early adulthood, I have had an unwritten list of my own of all the things I would like to do at least once. High on that list was a ride in a hot air balloon. One year my wife gave me a birthday gift of a hot air balloon ride. At the same time, Titus, my friend's wife gave him a similar birthday gift. We decided to go together. What may have prompted the idea, was a trip the four of us had taken to Colorado. We stopped off in Albuquerque, New Mexico, at their huge annual balloon festival where hundreds of balloons take flight. It was one of the most spectacular sights I have ever seen anywhere.

The day arrived with great anticipation. The launch was from the Quakertown Municipal Airport. We arrived early to watch them inflate the balloons. There were five balloons scheduled to lift off. The day was a balloonist's worse nightmare. It was extremely windy. The huge balloons were swirling in the wind making it almost impossible to inflate them without the fear of setting the balloon on fire. (Balloons are inflated by using high-powered fans blowing fire into the balloon to heat the air which causes the balloon to rise.) It appeared obvious that some, if not all the flights, would need to be aborted. After a period of time, three balloonists gave up the fight. However, our particular balloon seemed to be filling with hot air and slowly rising. There is a large woven basket, large enough for three adults, attached to the balloon with ropes. Three men were holding down the basket so it would not take off prematurely.

Suddenly, our balloonist called out for his two passengers. He yelled to us, "Climb in. Because of the wind we will take off like a rocket." We immediately climbed in. I had some difficulty, as I was too short and had to be pulled in. The balloonist told the men to let go and we shot straight up to a height of about 500 feet.

In the meantime, our son-in-law Jon, with the whole family aboard my van, decided to follow our flight. Because the flight plan was unpredictable, and the wind so strong, my family never had such a hair-raising trip in their lives.

We began to float very quickly. As soon as we were settled and floating leisurely along, our balloonist said to my friend and me, "Congratulations, you two are my first customers. I just passed my balloonist pilot license." I said, "Okay, we're even. This is our first hot air balloon ride too." Upon hearing the news that this was his maiden voyage as a licensed pilot, I immediately tightened my grip on the edge of the basket.

When riding in a balloon, the first thing you notice is no sense of motion. If you don't look down to the ground, you feel as though you are simply suspended in air. Because you move with the wind, there is no feeling of wind in your face as there would be on any other kind of locomotion. A conversation is just like you are all in the living room. The next thing you notice is the reaction of farm animals and dogs. They hear the sound of the balloonist occasionally employing his heater to keep hot air in the balloon. The animals react by wildly running in every direction.

Our flight plan took us over a sizeable lake. As we gently floated over the lake, the balloonist began to release the air in the balloon, and we began to descend. A small panic crept into my throat and I asked him what he was doing. He commented that it is customary when carrying rookie passengers, to drop the basket just inches into the water so the passengers can get their feet wet. We forcefully waived our right to this exercise so we hovered about 10 feet above the water. During the descent, it was amazingly quiet. A short distance from us was an old man who was fishing from an old row boat. He seemed oblivious to our presence. So I said, "Hi there, are you catching anything?" I feared the old guy was going to jump out of the boat. As he looked around and then looked up and saw this big balloon above his head, it scared much of the life out of him. Poor guy never responded.

As we were lifting off above the water, our balloonist also confessed that he did this to slow our balloon down behind a ridge. We had a one-hour flight scheduled, the passengers in the other balloon that had taken off with us had a thirty-minute flight. This gave the flight team that follows balloons time to pick up those passengers and proceed on to our destination. As we lifted off above the ridge, our balloon picked up considerable speed. We floated over a house where I could spot a man working on a large boat he had parked behind his house. I called out to him, "Hi, are you working hard?" He looked up and said, "Hi yourself, how is it going?" More often than I care to admit, I say some of the dumbest things imaginable. I said, "We're doing great but we're lost." How indescribably stupid is that? I saw him jump off his ladder, climb into his SUV and go flying out his driveway to follow us. Every once in a while, we could also catch a glimpse of Jon and the family in hot pursuit.

About this time, our balloonist announced that he would need to find a field suitable for landing the balloon. He spied an acceptable spot and slowly the balloon began its descent. As we were coming in at a high rate of speed, the balloonist warned of a very rough landing. He explained the wind would pull the basket along the ground until he could get all the air out of the balloon. He said, "Don't worry, just hang on." Boy, was that an understated forecast. It seemed like we were moving at thirty miles an hour when we hit. Immediately the basket tipped over. My friend and I now found ourselves lying on our stomachs on the side of the basket. Weeds and mud were coming at us like an avalanche. Would this race never end? Finally, the basket stopped. We rolled over and crawled out. We looked at each other and roared. There was mud and grass sticking out of every place I had an opening. About that time, both Jon and the man working on his boat arrived. I was embarrassed to explain we were not actually lost, although I had no idea where we were. He said he enjoyed the show and left. I understand it is customary for the balloonist to offer the owner of the land where the balloon comes down, a glass of champagne. Whether he did or not, I don't know. We left to clean up and rehearse the hot air balloon adventure.

A Boat + a Storm = Terror

CHAPTER 23

For many years, my family has enjoyed a summer home in Grasonville, on the eastern shore of Maryland. The house is situated on a tributary of the Chester River, an integral part of the Chesapeake Bay. This house has always had a special place in our family. My wife and I have seen our children grow up there and now enjoy the grandchildren growing up there too. We have reached the third generation with the birth of our great-grandson. It has been very special for us to have an active part in the development of their character. Two of our grandchildren have proposed marriage in the atmosphere of this place. Our great-grandson was given the name of Riley Grason in honor of this significant place.

As one might expect, the water became part of what we enjoyed. Fishing, and all kinds of water sports were commonplace. We had several small boats for fishing and skiing, but our primary family boat was a 28-foot cabin cruiser. We enjoyed family cruising in and around Annapolis, the Solomons, St. Michaels and beyond.

One warm summer evening, my wife and I were entertaining guests for the weekend. Glyn and Rita are more than just good friends; their son married our daughter. Neither Glyn nor Rita are nautical but we suggested taking the boat and going for dinner at a local restaurant built on the water, a short trip of about one and one-half nautical miles from our house. The restaurant is situated on a place called The Narrows, a narrow channel that connects the mighty Chester River to the lower part of the Chesapeake Bay. The ride over was delightful and thoroughly enjoyed by our guests. The water was like glass and a warm and gentle breeze made the trip very pleasant. We docked, went into the restaurant, enjoyed the meal and the company. We lingered over dinner and then decided it was time to board and head for home.

As soon as I came out of the restaurant, I sensed something was terribly wrong. This area is the center of local and tourist activity, with restaurants, dockside bars, moored boats and a beehive of people. First, there were no boats moving. The dockside bars had closed and were shuttered. Something very unusual was going on. I instructed my party to board quickly. My wife, having had ample experience on the water, also knew there was something very wrong. She tried to assure our guests that we would be home very soon. I instructed the three of them to stay below, while I would captain from the fly bridge. As soon as we started through the channel toward home, I saw significant streaks of lightning up ahead. The wind was picking up dramatically, but we were somewhat sheltered by buildings on either side of the channel.

As soon as we left the channel and hit open water, we encountered the storm in all of its fury. We learned later, a severe northeaster storm was approaching our area. Radio and television was broadcasting the news to get off the water. At no time during the day or evening was there any hint for us to know of what was to come.

The storm was coming out of the north, and my course was east. The gigantic waves hit the port (left) side of the boat with full force. The boat was listing from the port side to the starboard side in a moment. It was almost impossible to hold the wheel; I was hanging on the railing. My immediate fear was capsizing. I could hear the people below being thrown around like pinballs. I heard a scream as the cabin door slammed shut on Rita's thumb. My wife reported all three were petrified with fear. They feared I would be thrown overboard.

I knew we could not continue our charted course. I turned to the south and was carried along precipitously by the storm. The wind was at gale force. Thunder was deafening and continuous. The lightning was the kind we used to watch from the safety of our house, but this was vastly different. Along the water, lightning intensifies. It lights up the ground like giant spotlights. I knew there were several houses along the coast, and the credo of the sea is "any port in a storm." I set my heading in a southwesterly direction toward shore. Several hundred yards ahead I saw a dock that extended out into the bay. I headed for it. The storm had intensified now to where it was impossible to captain the boat. My hope was that I could keep the boat on the north side of the dock, so that the wind would push the boat against the dock, and we could use the dock for anchoring.

As we approached the dock, I saw two people coming out of the house—a woman and her teenage daughter. We learned later, the husband was afraid to venture out. (So much for manhood.) The rain was coming down in sheets, blowing sideways. The lightning was continuous. While the lightning was frightening, it helped us to see more clearly. The woman was calling but it was impossible to hear. She motioned for me to throw a bow line which I did. She secured the line to the bumper of their parked jeep. I attempted to secure a line at the stern. I decided I needed to get off the boat and attempt to further secure the boat. I timed my leap as the boat was going up and down. Standing on the dock, I was holding on to the bow rail of the boat. The waves were so high, I was lifted off the dock. Even though the boat was secured, the boat was rising up with each broadside wave. Each time it came down, it came down on a piling that was puncturing huge holes in the hull. My wife was screaming for me to let go of the boat for fear I would get crushed between the dock and the boat. Our guests were frightened beyond description and wanted to get off the boat. Under these conditions, I could not imagine how I could get them off safely.

With great difficulty and by the grace of God, we got the three of them off. Rita had her hand wrapped in a towel. Her thumb was severely injured. I watched for a moment as the pilings were making larger and larger holes in the side. Fortunately, most of the holes were above the water line. The three of them were invited into the house and after I had done all I could do, I too went in and called my family back at the house. They were worried and in great distress. They came, picked us up and took us to the hospital in Easton, Maryland. The medics bandaged Rita's thumb. We were amazed at the people lying on gurneys or otherwise waiting to be treated who had been struck by lightning.

I went back the next day to view the boat, and it was an awful sight. Huge holes all along the port side. We towed the boat to the nearest marina and waited for the insurance adjusters to inspect the damage. The boat was basically beyond repair and the insurance company settled the claim with me. I was surprised and disappointed with the man of the house where we had tied up. Not only did he refuse to come out to help us, but he called the next morning claiming some damage to his pilings. Jon, our son-in-law and I went back that morning and tried to repair damage we could not even find. There was no damage, only evidence of some fiberglass from the boat embedded into the top of the piling. I have always had great respect for the water and the weather that seems to change so quickly around the bay. We learned a lot that day! It is not good to fool with Mother Nature. She can be a demanding parent!

This Is Fur Enough

CHAPTER 24

Have you ever had a "cramp?" These cowardly beasts usually attack in the middle of the night when you least expect it. When they hit, you are catapulted out of bed, hop around the room on one leg like you're on a pogo stick, desperately trying to dislodge the affected part from the functioning part of your body. (By the way, when other people get them, they are kind of fun to watch.)

To prove that reasonably intelligent people are capable of doing some incredibly stupid things, I'll tell you about a "cramp" I had soon after we were married. This cramp did not attack my calf, or my ankle; no, this cramp attacked the non-functioning part of my body called the brain. I wasn't satisfied with just one brain cramp. Oh no, I had multiple cramps as you will see. This story is so embarrassing I don't think it should be reduced to writing. Maybe you should just call me!

Soon after our marriage, I went to work for a dairy as a milkman, a job I thoroughly enjoyed which says a lot about me. I would recommend this vocation to anyone who enjoys getting up at 2:30 a.m., walking all day carrying 8 quarts of milk at a time, in snow up to your chin, in weather in the single digits below zero. The mailmen, those weenies, wait for us to open the roads. But I digress!

It was the practice of my dairy for milkmen to work six days a week but only get paid for five days. Then every sixth week you would get a week off with pay. I absolutely loved it! Some of my friends got one week's vacation a year; I got one every six weeks. However, the problem that developed was what to do on these weeks off that was constructive. I was searching for an outlet when it happened.

In one of my sport magazines, there was an article that intrigued me. They reported that the fashion industry was turning to a new fur to replace the more expensive fur now being used, mink. This new fur was extremely soft like mink, but it was more durable than mink, and the animals were much easier to raise and were more prolific. The new fur was called nutria. We began to see fashion advertisements featuring the new fur, women of fashion were bedecked with flowing fur coats of nutria. A whole new fur industry had been born.

The article went on to state that there was one problem— too few ranchers raising nutria. After a minimal amount of research on my part, I contacted the author of the article and received an immediate response. Nutria require limited care, are vegetarians and thrive on produce the grocery stores throw away. The pens to house the nutria are easily constructed (not true) and a light began to shine in my non-functioning brain. We were assured there was a ready market for the pelts of full-grown nutria. Nevermind that I had zero experience raising anything except trouble.

Subsequently, we were contacted by two young men who were appointed as contact people for the nutria industry in the southeastern part of Pennsylvania. They came to interview us and we tried to make a good first impression. What wonderful and caring parents we would be to these cash machines called nutria. There were three obstacles we faced: One was the comment by these young men that the building lot on which our house was situated might be ultimately too small. The way these animals reproduce would require more room than we had. We needed to consider the possibility that we would need to relocate. That thought was not pleasant since my wife and I thought we would live in this house forever. The second obstacle was the price of the first breeding pair. The initial cost was $2000. In the mid 50's, I equated $2000 to be the equivalent to the national budget deficit. We would need to take out an equity loan of $3000 for the whole project. The third obstacle was approval by the zoning authority in Franconia Township.

Here is where my brain "cramp" flourished. Without nearly enough forethought, I signed up, subject only to approval of a loan and the approval of Franconia Township. The Township approved, for which I have never forgiven them, and my loan application was also approved. Thus we began this ill-fated enterprise. In preparation for their arrival, I received the plans for pen construction. I did not know nutria were aquatic. We had to provide swimming pools for them. That substantially increased the cost of construction. There were to be only two animals to each pen, and I only had room for three other pens. After an incredible amount of work and cost, far exceeding our budget for these pens, we notified the company we were ready for that loving couple.

The day of our adoption arrived. The newlyweds moved into their new home. I didn't realize how big they were—the size of a full-grown ground hog. I was thinking cuddly! What followed was a 24/7 operation and infinitely more work and worry than I had expected. After a period of months, our sweet couple was still childless. I inquired about this lack of family life and was assured once the pair was adjusted to each other, things would improve. I watched them carefully. I saw no love attraction whatsoever. One sat in one corner, the other in the far corner. I concluded we must have a fertility problem. It could be any one of the following: (A) The pair had sworn themselves to celibacy, (B) We had two of one kind (I wasn't about to check, I didn't even know where to look), or (C) They each lacked the core root of affection. I tried everything. Soft music, gentle words of encouragement, all to no avail.

Finally, brilliance was born out of desperation. I showed them a pick ax and threatened bodily harm.

About a year later, with still no nutria babies to call our own, the entire nutria industry had fallen on hard times. It was discovered women still preferred mink, and the nutria industry died. We requested the two young men come and claim their own nutria which they were reluctant to do. I found out they lost more money than we did. We lost well in excess of $3000 which was a blow of monumental proportions to our financial well-being.

One of the valuable lessons I learned from this fiasco was that "with age comes wisdom, but sometimes age just comes alone."

Martin Century Farms.

Our charming childless couple.

The Misadventures of a Milkman

CHAPTER 25

As I have indicated earlier in this book, I spent about eleven years as a milkman for a local dairy. First, as a deliveryman and then later I moved into a supervisor position. I must say that I enjoyed every minute of the business, it was the hours that could get you down. Since I am an early riser, I found the beautiful sunrises invigorating. I also enjoyed going home while everyone else was going to work.

My first assignment was a milk route in lower Bucks County. Since it was on the outer reaches of our serving area, I was assigned the oldest truck. The company was so ashamed of this truck, they kept the name of a defunct dairy on the side of this truck. The only thing I liked about this truck was its lack of speed. The truck was so slow that at top speed, I could steer with my knees and do the mandatory book work while driving back to the dairy. The logic was, that if I ran into anything, they probably wouldn't notice. After a successful year, I was transferred to a more local area and given a "Divco" truck. This was a fascinating but challenging experience. In this truck, you drove standing up. The accelerator was on the floor, the clutch and the brake was the same pedal. For the clutch, you pushed the pedal down halfway. If you pushed down too far you slammed on the brakes.

As you might imagine, the learning process was painful. I would hit the brake when I attempted to shift gears, slamming my body into the steering wheel. This was also the time when the milk bottles would cry out and some would surrender, leaving me to explain how I got milk in my shoes. However, this "Divco" had one redeeming quality. The locking brake was a lever that could be pulled and locked. When I learned the idiosyncrasies of my truck, I could pull the brake lever, grab two quarts of milk, jump out and know that the truck would continue down the street to the next stop. It was similar to a horse who knew the route.

As you might surmise, this job was great in good weather, but it was not at all pleasant when the weather turned bad. My stories are legion about snowstorms and inclement weather. I will relate just a few.

When severe weather was predicted, I would spend the night at my mother's home situated on a main road. Many times I would lie in bed and sense a blizzard was in progress. In these times, (like three o'clock in the morning), lying in my warm bed and knowing what lay ahead of me this day, I would recall my pastor talking about the return of Jesus at an hour when we think not. I tried to use my theological power to suggest to Him that this would be an excellent time. Failing that, I would get up, put on everything I owned and venture into the inevitable. On one such occasion, as I was traveling to the dairy in extremely heavy snow, the electric lines were down, consequently there were no traffic lights. At an intersection near the dairy, another car was approaching from my right. He couldn't stop and hit my car. We both spun around, sustained significant damage but thankfully no one was injured. The police came and I needed to explain this leather sack full of money, which was in my possession, that I used in the course of the business. When the police checked on the other driver, he was arrested for the illegal possession of a handgun. The police took him away and called another police-man to take me to the dairy. What a great start for the day.

On another occasion, the snow had been falling heavily all evening. The snowplows were busy but could not keep up. I got up at two o'clock and got into my car to see if I could get to the main road. The snow was covering my headlights and I could see nothing. All of a sudden, I hit a huge snowdrift and came to a full and complete stop. I could barely get out of my car. As I did, I could just make out an abandoned car that had hit the same snowdrift but coming from the opposite direction. I soon realized what could have happened.

I walked back to the house, probably a quarter of a mile, called the dairy and told them I was snowed in. I was told to walk out to the main road and they would pick me up with their truck. I walked about a mile in snow up to my waist. I waited and waited but no one showed up. I walked back to my house and called again. It was now after 4:00 a.m. I was told that the truck had gotten stuck but I should walk out again since they just dug it out. I walked out again in the midst of a blinding blizzard, was picked up and taken to the dairy to begin my day. I returned to the dairy so late that night, I along with several other guys slept on the floor at the dairy so we would be available the next day.

I want to tell you another weather related story that is much funnier now than it was when it happened. I had agreed to serve as the best man at a wedding and asked to have the day off but was told that would be impossible. However, I would be permitted to take a helper with me as long as the helper was an employee of the dairy. As it happened, I had a good friend, Art York, who was employed by the dairy and worked in the plant. He also was to be part of the wedding.

I got up at two o'clock to a flood. It had been raining most of the day before and it was coming down in sheets. I met Art at the dairy and we started out. I was directing traffic telling Art to grab two quarts of milk and run it to this house while I ran all over the neighborhood dispensing milk. Needless to say, we were drenched and I wished we had life jackets. The streets were flooding and the outlook was not good. Then it happened. Pointing to a certain house, I said, "Art, jump out and take a couple of quarts of milk to that house." Art jumped out and disappeared. He had jumped directly into a storm sewer. As he crawled out sputtering and spitting, I asked him what happened to the milk. He saw little humor in that question. The good news was that he was not any wetter than he was prior to his swim. The bad news was that we made it to the wedding! Just kidding!

• • • • •

After a number of successful years as a route milkman, I was promoted to the position of Supervisor of Sales. I joined about five other men who held similar positions. I was responsible for twenty route men plus four route foremen. To say my first day as a supervisor was eventful is a gross understatement. I arrived at the dairy, no longer dressed in a milkman's uniform but a business suit and tie. Right inside the front door of the sales department was a floor to ceiling mirror. At the top of the mirror was a sign "This Is What Your Customers See." I studied myself in the mirror and I concluded I looked great.

When I arrived at my desk, there was a note requesting a meeting at 9:00 a.m. sharp in the office of my sales manager. I assumed it was a courtesy call welcoming me into the world of middle management. It wasn't! Present in addition to the manager was the company comptroller, a man I had never met. After brief pleasantries the comptroller said, "Bob, we have reason to believe one of your route men is an embezzler. We need you to investigate, and if confirmed, he must be dismissed today." I inquired as to which man it was and acknowledged I had never met him. I told both men I would look into the matter and report back to them but I had no idea what to do next. I walked out of the office on very wobbly knees. I sat down at my desk to reflect on what just happened and to question this promotion. I had no experience in this kind of responsibility.

I decided my best course of action was to meet this route man out on the job. I drove out to his area, found the dairy truck and jumped in. The route man was coming down the sidewalk, and was very surprised to see me. I thought he did appear quite tense. As he got into the truck, I stuck out my hand, introduced myself as his new supervisor, and he acknowledged he had received the news. We exchanged some small talk. I asked him about his family (as I recall he had two sons) and how things were going for him. He responded "good." I told him what I expected from my route men and that I was available to help him in any way I could. We shook hands again and I left. Back at the dairy I waited for him to return. I was very uneasy and nervous. When he arrived about mid-afternoon I waited for him to park his truck and invited him to join me in the drivers' conference room. It was there I intended to confront him.

He was a much bigger man than I (who isn't) and my manager had several guys outside the conference door in case of any altercation. I started by telling him the company comptroller had spoken to me about the unusually high accounts receivable on his route. Could he explain why this seems to be a problem. Almost immediately he began to break down, eyes filled with tears and he confessed to stealing money. He explained he was gambling and hoping to make it big and then he would replace the money. After a period of time, I asked him to remain and I left to convey the confession to my supervisor. I went back into the room and told him he was terminated effective immediately. What I didn't know was my sales manager, in an attempt to make an example of this route man, had called the police and with their lights flashing took the man away in handcuffs. I sure hoped my days as a supervisor would get better than this first one!

I must share one more story that became a legend. One of my route foreman was deathly afraid of dogs—big ones, little ones, quiet ones, loud barking ones—all kinds of dogs petrified him. Because he only served this particular route occasionally, he was unfamiliar with the different customers and their unique circumstances. This one customer was standing at the door when my foreman pulled up. They had a small dog that was in the yard. As soon as my foreman got out of the truck, this little dog approached him and became very aggressive. The customer told my foreman to pick up the morning newspaper lying on the drive and make believe he was going to hit the dog and he would run away. Here is where the story has two explanations. The customer claims my foreman hit the dog so hard that it later died. My foreman told me the dog had snapped at his heels and he was just doing what the customer told him he could do. The legend has it that my foreman put a small pipe or stick of some kind inside the newspaper and inflicted a lethal blow. I spoke with my foreman who made no confession regarding a pipe or a stick but stood by his story and was completely unrepentant. The customer demanded full restitution for the dog. We made satisfactory compensation and the story ended, but not too well.

Where's the Beef

CHAPTER 26

I readily admit to my abject failure as a nutria rancher as confirmed by my report in Chapter 24. However, that is not the sum total of the entire account. Here is the rest of the story:

Our residence was situated on two acres of ground and since we no longer needed the land for the failed nutria business, I had a decision to make with respect to all that ground. I could keep it all in lawn but I hated to see my wife mowing two acres of grass. After all, I do have some compassion. At our original house, the lawn was much smaller. I would be sitting in our air conditioned house, watching the Phillies on TV, and looking out of the window, I could see my wife mowing, trimming, and sweating. It was hard to watch. The solution: close the blinds. Good news, in no time, the guilty feeling goes away. However, since I still had rancher blood coursing through my veins, I decided to build a fence on the rear portion of the lot giving me a one-acre pasture. I was going into the cattle business. I subsequently erected a small barn.

My story continues: In those days, there was a livestock auction held weekly in a neighboring town. Here the farmers would bring in excess livestock to be purchased by ranchers, dairy farmers, and those in the retail and wholesale meat business. So,

I attended one of these auctions and purchased a newly-weaned black Angus calf. I carried that calf to my car, tied all four legs together and placed the calf in the trunk. I became a tender loving mother to that new member of our family. For the first few nights, that calf slept like a baby—it cried all night. I had to mix a formula and teach the calf how to drink milk. I would put about four to six inches of the milk formula in a bucket, then put my hand in the milk formula and let the calf suck on my two fingers in order to teach this child how to learn to feed itself. This calf grew through good food, tender loving care, pleasant environment and no global warming.

The plot thickens: Once a year, Pennsylvania holds a giant farm show in Harrisburg for thousands of people. It is a farmer's extravaganza. All vendors selling anything vaguely related to farming are represented. It was a tradition each year that two friends, Titus Hendricks, Art York and I would make the farm show a guys' day out. I had just begun my cattle business, i.e. one calf, when the three of us attended the farm show. We were strolling down the aisle in the feed and fertilizer department of the show. There was a large and very prominent display for Beacon Feed. Unknown to me, one of my two friends had run ahead and told the man from Beacon Feed that I was in the cattle business, had a huge operation and he would do well to try to sell me on Beacon Feed. As I came by, he stopped me and asked if I raised cattle. I wasn't sure one 50-pound calf could be considered cattle but I wasn't going to quibble over numbers, so I said yes.

He began to extol the many virtues of Beacon Feed. He began to emphasize that not only is Beacon Feed the best on the market but their delivery service was second to none. He asked if I was buying my feed in bulk. I said no but I lacked the nerve to tell him I was buying my feed in 10-pound paper bags. At this point, I looked over at my friends and saw they were doubled over in acute pain from laughing at me and my interview. Now I knew I had been duped. Quickly, my mind began to explore my options. The option I chose was this one: I became very interested in Beacon Feed. How quickly could a Beacon Feed representative come to my ranch? How much notice must be given for a one-ton bulk delivery! I was assured a representative could come by within days and one week notice was all that was needed for bulk delivery. I expressed my keen interest in Beacon and hoped we could have a long-term working relationship. The man readily agreed. I told him, "Since I am very busy, please call first before you come or before any delivery of bulk feed." He assured me they would call first to be sure I was home. I left the Beacon display and gave the representative the phone number and home address of Art York.

• • • • •

Have you ever found yourself laughing when you see someone slip and fall? Why is it that we often find that funny? I am not talking about a serious injury, I mean the kind of stumble and fall that is more embarrassing than dangerous. That is what this next story is all about. No, it wasn't I who slipped and fell! If it had been me, this story would not have appeared in these pages. But let me tell you about it, but please show restraint in your laughing out of respect. The man who is the subject of this story didn't think it was that funny.

After a few years of successfully raising steers for our meat supply, I received a call from my father-in-law. He asked if my pasture would support two steers? I assured him it would. He said, "Bob, I have a business proposal to offer." I replied, "Great, what is?" He said, "I will supply two yearling steers, and I will pay all the expenses for both animals. When they reach the age where we can have them slaughtered: there will be one for your family and one for mine." I could hardly turn down an offer like that. Several weeks later, a cattle truck pulled into my driveway and on the truck were two yearling steers. One was a black angus which I preferred, the other was a white-faced Hereford, a breed my father-in-law preferred. The whole process went well with the one exception—that black angus of mine had the wanderlust. If he searched for a weakness in the fence, and found it, he exploited it and he would get out. There were times of enormous frustration as we tried to corral him back into the pasture.

After a number of months, the two steers were into the 800- to 900-pound range, too early to be considered prime. One morning I went out to the barn to find the Hereford laying on his side with all four legs in the same direction. Very unusual for a steer to lay like that. They usually fold their legs under themselves when they lay down. Later that day, I checked again and he had not moved. I tried to get him up but he wouldn't budge. Early the next morning, I went out to the barn to find the steer in the same spot. Obviously he had nothing to eat or drink. I called the veterinarian, explained the matter and he said he would stop over. When he arrived, he could not find anything seriously wrong with the animal and concluded the steer may have ingested a foreign object he picked up in the pasture. This could be a very serious matter. Together, the veterinarian and I tried to get the steer on his feet, but without success.

I was advised by the doctor to wait until the morning, and if he had not moved on his own, the doctor recommended we make arrangements for immediate slaughter. You could lose the animal altogether. I called my father-in-law to apprise him of the situation and of the veterinarian's recommendation.

The next morning there was no change and the steer looked very lethargic. I called a local slaughterhouse and they were prepared to handle the case. I called the livestock hauler and told him of the emergency. He said, "I can't come now personally but I will send my father who helps out in cases like this." I replied, "Fine, but please hurry."

A short time later, a truck pulled in to the barn, and a short elderly gentleman got out of the truck. He immediately took charge. He put a halter over the steer's head with a long rope attached. He then began to pull and I pushed and kicked until finally the steer had had enough and slowly tried to get up. Once on his feet, I suggested we let him stand for a moment before we try to get him on board. After a few minutes, the old man began to pull on the rope. Slowly the steer began to move.

Then the most amazing and totally unexpected thing happened. The steer bolted and took off across the pasture. The old man was holding on to the rope and was gaining speed as they headed for the back fence. The old man, true to his calling, did not let go of the rope. He was being dragged along on his stomach. He lost his hat and his glasses. (We later found both.) I was in hot pursuit hoping the steer would stop at the fence, which he did. I arrived at the scene in time to see the old man covered with mud and grass on his coveralls and in his teeth. Watching this scene take place, was one of the funniest things I had ever seen. I was embarrassed, but I was laughing uncontrollably. What happened next was priceless! The old man rolled over on his side and was attempting to get up. While laughing, I reached my hand to help him up and as I did so, the old man looked at me and said, "What did you say was wrong with this animal?"

But now we had a decision to make. I called my father-in-law and told him to decide if he thought this was a miracle recovery or an aberration. He opted to have our original plan be carried out. I'm sorry to report that I have not yet been cured from my tendency to laugh at inappropriate times.

A Few Regrets
CHAPTER 27

My life has been rich with experiences and filled with glorious opportunities, and if I had a "do-over," I would probably make the same mistakes again, but I would enjoy the privilege. But in this process of life, there are a few regrets that come to mind. For example:

I regret that I was not born left-handed. People who are left-handed seem to have more fun. The achievement bar is set low for persons who are left-handed. Not that much is expected from them. They just go on to become Presidents of the United States and do other dumb things. I think I would have enjoyed being left-handed and I think I would have been pretty good at it.

I regret missing my mid-life crisis. I was at the gym that afternoon pumping iron. When I got home, my wife told me it was over, and I was too late. I read a lot about male mid-life crisis, and it certainly sounded intriguing. I'm really sorry I missed it. I learned a valuable lesson about life from that experience. Don't be wasting time at the gym when you could be enjoying your birthright.

I regret being born so late. My parents were very shy! I would like to have been born at a time before Sir Isaac Newton invented gravity. It would have been interesting to live with everything and everybody suspended. I mean, if you lost weight, where would it go? Would it just hang around? Could you throw a ball? Would it ever stop? Could they catch it? Think about it! This is important stuff. I think Isaac should have invented something else, like maybe edible broccoli.

I regret that my wife didn't marry higher in the human chain! She is a great person who never complains about her lot in life and she does deserve better. Maybe I should introduce her to somebody important.

I regret I didn't study harder when I was in school. In high school, I majored in tennis and minored in absentia. My best friend was smart enough for the both of us. He planned to go on to college; I didn't plan to do anything. But if I were to go into business, I told him, "When you graduate from college, come see me. I'll hire you. I want the smartest employees I can get."

I regret there is so much time and so little to do!

And finally, I regret that I have been born with an excessive amount of humility. I find humility to be like a millstone around my neck. It prevents people from knowing how great I really am. Sorry for your loss!

A Last Laugh

CHAPTER 28

Since the premise of this book is that laughter has real medicinal value and makes us feel good about ourselves, I wanted to include in the book some of my personal favorite stories. Enjoy!

• • • • •

A ninety-year-old woman gave birth to a baby, thanks to medical technology. She agreed to be interviewed and invited the press to visit her and see the baby. Local, national and TV news invaded her house. After the interview, they asked to see the baby. "Not yet," was the mother's response. After more questions, the press asked again if they could see the baby. Again the mother said, "No, not yet." Somewhat perplexed, the press asked, "When can we see this baby?" The mother replied, "As soon as she cries! I can't remember where I put her!"

• • • • •

One fellow walked into the doctor's office, and the receptionist asked what he had. "Shingles," he said. She took his name, address and insurance information and told him to take a seat. Fifteen minutes later, a nurse's aide came out and asked him what he had. "Shingles," he replied. She took down his height, weight, complete medical history and told him to wait in the examining room. A half hour later, a nurse came into the examining room and asked him what he had. "Shingles," the man said. The nurse gave him a blood test, took his blood pressure and did an electrocardiogram. Then she told him to strip down to his underwear. She said, "The doctor will be in soon." One hour later, the doctor arrived and asked him what he had. "Shingles," the man said. The doctor asked, "Where?" "Outside on my truck. Where do you want them?"

• • • • •

A little boy from the second grade came home from school and asked his mother for a quarter. His explanation: My teacher is leaving and we are giving her a little momentum.

• • • • •

Two men crashed their plane on a South Pacific island. Both survived. One of the men, after brushing himself off, proceeded to run all over the island to see if they had any chance of survival. He rushed back to the other man screaming, "This island is uninhabited. There is no food, no water, we are going to die here." The other man leaned back against the fuselage of the wrecked plane, folded his arms and responded, "No we're not going to die, I make $100,000 a week." The first man grabbed his friend, shook him and said, "Listen, I'm telling you, there is no food and there is no water. We are done!" Again, the man, unruffled, said, "I told you, we'll be fine. I make $100,000 each week."

Mystified, the first man repeated, that without food and water, they were going to die. Finally, the second man looked his frustrated friend in the eye and said, "Look, I make $100,000 every week. I tithe my income to the church. Believe me, my pastor will find us."

• • • • •

The CEO of Smith Foods, a large poultry distributor, met with the head of a large church. He said, "My company will donate $500,000 to your church if you change the Lord's prayer from 'Give us this day, our daily bread' to 'Give us this day our daily chicken.' The pastor responded, "That's impossible. The Lord's prayer is fixed and cannot be changed." The CEO replied, "We will increase our offer to one million dollars." Later, the pastor met with his elders and said, "I have good news and bad news. The good news is the church is receiving a check from Smith Foods for one million dollars. The bad news is we will be losing the Wonder Bread account."

• • • • •

Len died. His widow thought she should put a notice of his passing in the obituary column of the local newspaper. The newspaper employee asked, "What do you want to say?" The woman said, "Len died." "Is that all you want to say about your husband's passing? Surely you could say more than just 'Len died.' If it is a matter of cost, let me tell you the first five words are free." The woman thought for awhile and then said, "Okay, add 'Boat For Sale'."

• • • • •

A loud pounding on the door at 3:00 a.m. awakened a man and his wife. The man got up and went downstairs to find a drunken stranger at the door asking for a push. "Are you crazy?" the man said. "It's 3:00 a.m. I'm not giving anybody a push at this hour," and he slammed the door. After explaining what the pounding on the door was and his response, his wife said, "Don't you remember when we broke down on our vacation and those two guys went out of their way to help us? I really think you should go down and give the man a push."

Begrudgingly, the husband got dressed and went down to help the man. Opening the door, he couldn't see anyone. He called out, "Hello, are you still here?" "Yes," came an answer. "Do you still need a push?" "Yes, thanks." "Where are you?" the husband asked. "Over here, on the swing."

• • • • •

A kindergarten teacher gave each child a piece of paper and a crayon and told each child to draw anything he or she would like. One little girl began immediately and was very intent on what she was drawing. Fascinated by her zeal, the teacher went to the little girl and asked, "What are you drawing?" Without looking up, she replied, "I'm drawing a picture of God." The teacher said, "Honey, nobody has seen God. No one knows what He looks like." "They'll know in a minute" the little girl responded.

• • • • •

Two snakes were crawling along when one snake said to the other, "Are we poisonous?" The other snake responded, "Well, of course we're poisonous. We're rattlesnakes. Why do you ask?" The first snake said, "I just bit my tongue."

• • • • •

The mother of three boys who were totally out of control and unruly was asked if she had to do it all over again, would she have children? She replied, "Yes, I would. But not the same ones."

• • • • •

Two deacons decided to skip church one Sunday morning and get in a round of golf. Their games did not go well and bad soon became worse. One deacon said to the other, "Now, I feel guilty. I wish I had gone to church." The second deacon responded, "Well, I wouldn't have gone to church anyway. My wife is really sick in bed."

• • • • •

I'm really worried about my bank! They leave the door to the vault open but they chain the pen to the desk.

• • • • •

Do you know what would have happened if it had been three wise women instead of three wise men to see Jesus? They would first ask directions, then arrive on time, help to deliver the baby, clean the stable, make a casserole, give practical gifts, and there would be peace on earth.

My Epilogue

I have just finished reading the final draft of my first attempt at literary immortality. As I have relived the events about which I have written, some second guessing comes into play. Why did I decide to write this book? Did this book sound as though my life was something special that people needed to know? Did it seem as though I had all the answers to life's many and varied problems? Did I make it appear as though I had no problems, that my life was indeed just a bowl of cherries? That things always work out just right?

My friend, if that is the impression this book leaves, then I have failed miserably. For I decided to make this book a reality, partly because my family encouraged it, but also to hopefully challenge my readers to be positive in a negative world. I wanted the book to be fun to read, and yet be inspiring. I wanted this book to not only put a premium on laughter, but I also wanted to leave my readers uplifted, feeling better about themselves and happier for having had the experience. I truly hope I have done that!

I am paraphrasing what Jesus said in His Book, "I have come to give you life and if you will trust me, I will make your life better than you ever thought possible."

And finally, I have discovered that true happiness is not dependent on great happenings, but by enjoying the little things that make up life. I have enjoyed sharing my life with you.

Acknowledgments

The greatest Book ever written was not written by just one man. Neither was this book! I'm grateful to my wife, Mildred, and our two daughters, Kathy Delp and Patti Mangum, for their combined encouragement that has helped to make this venture a family affair; and to Laura Mangum, my grandson's bride who tirelessly labored to make the multitude of literary corrections required. To my entire family of grandchildren, who were kind enough to laugh at my stories, to be patient enough to wait through them, and encouraged me to reduce the stories to print: Jenna, Ryan, Kyle, Chad, and Tyler and their spouses: I love you all.

To friends, Mr. and Mrs. Norman Keller who graciously supplied much of the material for Australia and New Zealand, to Ronn Moyer and Pete Musselman, my good friends, who preceded me in writing a book. I learned much from their combined experience.

To the number of good friends whose names have been interspersed throughout this book! Like Arden and Shirley Keller, our traveling companions on many of these stories, and with whom we shared a vacation condo. We shared many happy memories with our long-time friends, Shirley and Titus Hendricks, and the passing of Titus continues to leave a void in our lives.

And to our dear friends, Glyn and Rita Mangum, our son-in-law's parents, with whom we shared many good times as well as the harrowing boat ride described in Chapter 23.

To Don and Jayne Dressler, and Marion Gibbon, who contributed so much to our enjoyment as we spent our days at the Rift Valley Academy in the fascinating country of Kenya.

And finally, a special note of thanks to Sharon Rousseau, my grandson's fiancé who skillfully guided me through the maze of computer challenges! Without her help, I would be writing this book in longhand.

As I have rehearsed these stories, I have been reminded of how rich Mildred and I are in old friends.

With much gratitude to you all, my prayer is that God will be pleased to bless each one of you!